GENTLEMEN OF THE FLASHING BLADE

STUDIES IN NORTH QUEENSLAND HISTORY

1. Anne Allingham, *'Taming the Wilderness': the first decade of pastoral settlement in the Kennedy District,* 2nd ed., 1978, rep. 1989.

2. Peter Bell, *The Mount Mulligan Disaster, 1921*, 1978; reprinted 1989.

3. Diane Menghetti, *The Red North: the Popular Front in north Queensla*nd, 1981, rep. 1989.

4. Christine Doran, *Separatism in Townsville, 1884 to 1894: 'We should govern ourselves',* 1981.

5. Dawn May, *From Bush to Station: aboriginal labour in the north Queensland pastoral industry, 1861-1897*, 1983.

6. Cathie May, *Topsawyers: the Chinese in Cairns, 1870-1920*, 1984.

7. Dorothy M. Gibson-Wilde, *Gateway to a Golden Land: Townsville to 1884*, 1984.

8. Anne Smith, *Roberts, Leu and North: a Centennial History*, 1986.

9. Dorothy M. Gibson-Wilde and Bruce Gibson-Wilde, *A Pattern of Pubs: Hotels of Townsville 1864-1914*, 1988.

10. Helen Brayshaw, *Well Beaten Paths: Aborigines of the Herbert Burdekin District, North Queensland. An Ethnography and Archaeology Study*, pp.336. Forthcoming.

11. Marjorie Pagani, *T.W. Crawford: Politics and the Queensland Sugar Industry*. 1990.

12. Bianka Vidonya Balanzategui, *Gentlemen of the Flashing Blade*. 1990.

13. Janice Wegner, *The Etheridge*. Forthcoming.

14. Christine Doran, *Partner in Progress: A History of Electricity Supply in* North *Queensland*. Forthcoming.

CANE CUTTING

Horses (seen here hauling out loaded trucks) were still used by some cane farmers in the late 1940s)

facing p.iii

GENTLEMEN OF THE FLASHING BLADE

Bianka Vidonja Balazategui

For the displaced person canecutters of my acquaintance -

true 'Gentlemen of the Flashing Blade'.

First published 1990 James Cook University

Second published 2015
Boolarong Press
655 Toohey Road
Salisbury Qld 4107
Australia
www.boolarongpress.com.au

National Library of Australia Cataloguing-in-Publication entry:

Creator:	Balanzategui, Bianka Vidonja, author.
Title:	Gentlemen of the flashing blade / Bianka Vidonja Balanzategui.
ISBN:	9781925236057 (paperback)
Subjects:	Sugar workers--Queensland--History.
	Sugarcane--Queensland--Harvesting--History.
	Sugarcane industry--Queensland--History.
Dewey Number:	338.1736109943

New Cover Design by Boolarong Press

Published by Boolarong Press, Salisbury, Brisbane, Australia.

Printed and bound by Watson Ferguson & Company, Salisbury, Brisbane, Australia.

FOREWORD

In this fine study of immigrant cane-cutters Bianka Vidonja Balanzategui has brought together two of the major themes of North Queensland history - immigration and the sugar industry. The two have always been related. The industry was founded by entrepreneurs, who although coming originally from the British Isles, had often had experience of sugar growing in other parts of the Empire. The first large labour force came from the islands of Vanuatu and the Solomons. But many other migrant groups worked in the industry - Japanese, Javanese, Italians. The first large scale immigration of Italians took place in 1891. The intention was to replace the Melanesian labour with indentured Italian labour.

The establishment of central mills and small family-owned farms created the need for teams of seasonal workers who could cut the cane when it was ready for harvest. The cane-cutter became, like the shearer, one of the key workers in Australia's great rural industries creating a highly distinctive life style, unique patterns of work and leisure and a rich folk-lore.

It was inevitable, with the labour shortages of the post-war period, that many of the new Australians would end up in the cane-fields of North Queensland. It was worlds away from what they had known in Europe. The adaptability, determination and fortitude of those young men from widely differing backgrounds is a story that needs to be told to present day Australians.

Bianka succeeds admirably in weaving together her two themes. This is a tribute to her literary skill and to her personal experience. Her father came from Slovenia, the northern-most part of Yugoslavia and joined the great exodus from war-torn Europe to Australia. Her childhood was dominated by the seasonal nature of the cane cutters life. She lived in the cane-barracks while the season lasted and then went south in the slack to attend many different primary schools in various parts of Australia. Her childhood was part of the way of life that she celebrates, a way of life that has passed into memory, history and legend.

Henry Reynolds

ACKNOWLEDGEMENTS

I acknowledge with heartfelt gratitude my father - a displaced person canecutter - a truly gentle man whose life of hard work, generosity and loving commitment to his family is inspiring. My father and mother's constant encouragement made this book possible.

My Balanzategui family too was magnanimous with its interest, time and help. The generosity shown me and trust invested in me by the displaced person interviewees and other contributors to this book are gratefully acknowledged.

Associate Professor Henry Reynolds cannot be ever thanked sufficiently for the patience and good-humour he showed in the hours of proof-reading and consultation that nuturing this book from infancy to maturity demanded.

Dr John Kennedy of the Reader Services Division, James Cook University Library and those staffs who processed my unnumerable inter-libary loan request I am particulary appreciative. Living outside of Townsville and writing on a very part-time basis meant that I was at times a difficult borrower!

Especial recognition must be made of author John Naish and his books: *The Clean Breast, The Cruel Field*, and *That Men Should Fear*. The expression: 'Gentlemen of the Flashing Blade', is his.

CONTENTS

Illustrations

Glossary of canecutting terms

Bin — See 'truck'.

Canecutter — A man who manually harvested sugar cane.

Cocky — Farmer.

Crows nesting — Loading cane onto a truck in a haphazard manner.

Cut-out — Particularly 'cut-out day', the final day of the season when the last stalk of cane a gang had been contracted to cut was harvested.

Dirty cane — Cane sent to the mill without trash and tops adequately removed.

Double-tiered — Stalks of short cane loaded so as to overlap in the centre of the truck.

Drill — A row of cane: drills are 4'7" apart.

Dummy — A man who signed on for another in his absence. Also an inexperienced man recruited into a gang to make up numbers and expected to leave at a later date.

Filestick — A length of pipe in which files were stored in the field.

Floaters — Flying burning cane leaves issuing from burning cane.

Fly gang — A gang which had fulfilled its contract and was sent by the Cane Inspector to another farm or into another district to help a gang which was behind its contract: 'flying' from one unfinished contract to another.

Gang — Group of canecutters contracted to a farmer to cut his cane.

Ganger — Leader of the gang.

Gun Cutter — The best cutter in a gang. A rare gang could be made up of 'gun' cutters and develop some renown.

Hairy-mary — Minute hair-like follicles covering cane leaves which easily become imbedded in the skin causing a rash.

Headland — Access road bordering a cane paddock.

Jacky Howe — A dark coloured singlet frequently worn by the canecutter and identified with the canecutter in popular imagination.

Rake — A quantity of cane harvested in one cutting session which and to be loaded before cutting recommenced.

Retention money — A small amount of money deducted from the canecutter's fortnightly pay and reimbursed on completion of his contract, as an inducement to fulfill the contract.

Season — The months spent canecutting: usually June to December.

Sign-on	The signing of the contract between farmer and gang, marking the start of the season.
Single-tiered	Stalks of long cane loaded so as to lie across the entire width of the truck.
Slack	The five months between harvest seasons.
Smoko	Breaks from work in mid-morning and mid-afternoon.
Stool	A clump of cane stalks originating as shoots growing from one bud at a node.
Top	Green leaves and cabbage (green, soft length where the leaves branch out from the stalk).
Topping	Cutting off the tops.
Tram	Subdivision of a paddock for convenience in cutting: each contained approximately 18 drills of cane.
Trash	Dry cane leaves removed by burning or by use of the hook on the end of the cane knife.
Truck	(Later called 'bin'). The wheeled receptacle onto which cane was loaded to be hauled by locomotive to the mill.

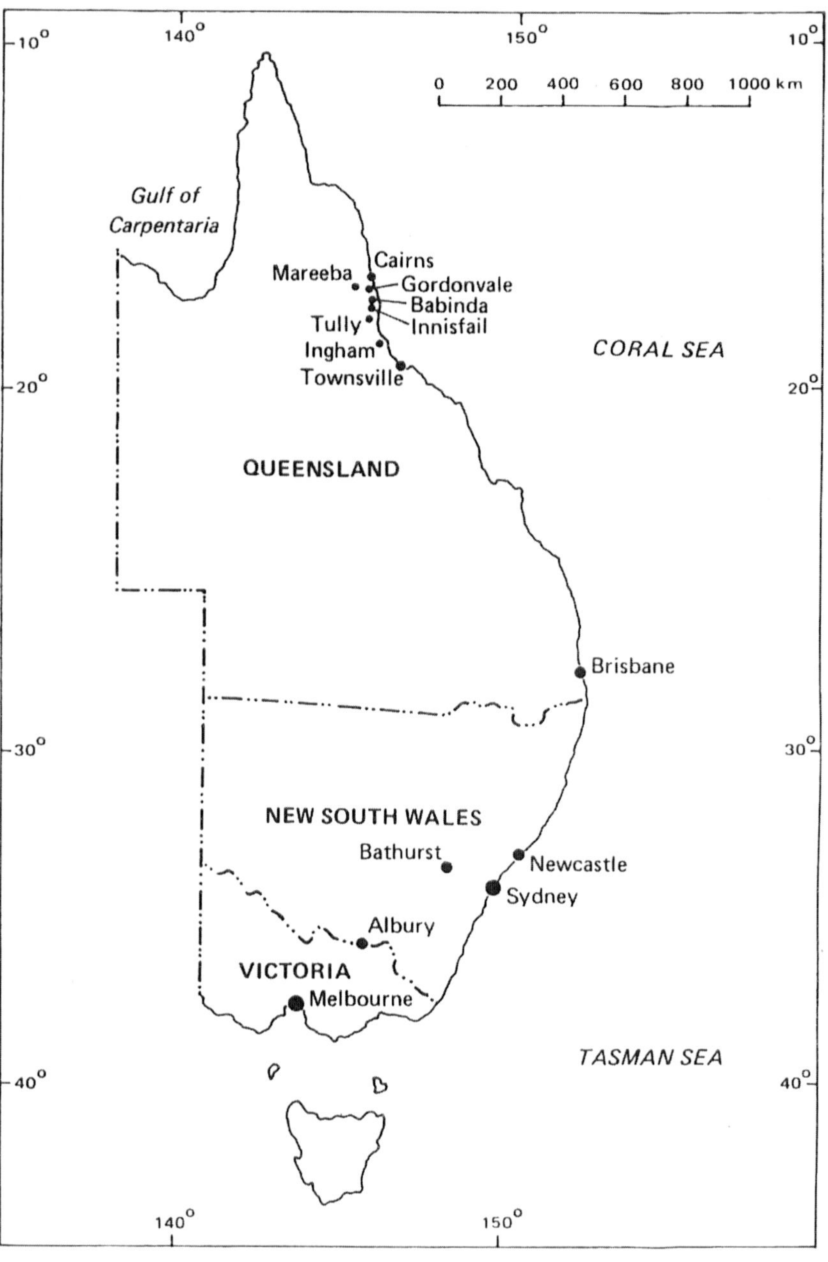
10°
140°
150°
10°
0
200
400
600
800
1000 km
Gulf of Carpentaria
Cairns
Mareeba
Gordonvale
Babinda
Tully
Innisfail
Ingham
Townsville
CORAL SEA
20°
20°
QUEENSLAND
Brisbane
30°
30°
NEW SOUTH WALES
Bathurst
Newcastle
Sydney
Albury
VICTORIA
Melbourne
TASMAN SEA
40°
40°
140°
150°

INTRODUCTION

The displaced survivors of World War II were one of its most tragic legacies. Mourning fellow countrymen, many of whom had been decimated, they felt that they could not safely or happily return to their home countries which had undergone cataclysmic changes of frontiers, sovereignty and political structure. Between nine and 12 million non-German displaced people comprising soldiers, forced labourers, political deportees, prisoners of war and fugitives were dispersed throughout Europe at the close of the war. After repatriation of the greater proportion, there remained a significant number who for various reasons could not, or would not, return to their countries of origin.

In the period 1 July 1947 to 31 December 1951, approximately two million of these were found new homes by an organization created especially for this purpose: the International Refugee Organization (I.R.O.). The first international agency created by the United Nations Organization, the I.R.O. was described by its last Director General as "the most successful example of large-scale international co-operation for humanitarian purposes in history".[1]

In July 1945, the newly created portfolio of Immigration in the Australian federal government was bestowed upon Arthur A. Calwell. As Minister for Immigration he launched Australia upon an ambitious immigration programme unprecedented in its history. As a member of the United Nations Australia automatically assumed membership of the I.R.O. and agreed in June, 1947 to become the recipient of displaced person migrants. Though the necessity for the programme was expressed in diverse ways, perhaps the most valid justification was that the scale of labour required for post-war industrial recovery and expansion could not be met by the Australian populace alone. Although British immigrants were regarded as ideal, 170,000 displaced persons were admitted into Australia among the 572,300 migrants who arrived by December 1951.

Factors which hampered substantial British migration to Australia did not impede the migration of displaced persons. The I.R.O. facilitated their migration and for Australia it was both a humanitarian gesture which would be globally approved as helping to solve an international problem, and a move of economic value in an era of accelerated industrial development.

All displaced persons were admitted under 'Certificate of Exemption'[2] which compelled them, under threat of deportation, to remain in approved occupations for two years. This contract meant that they could be directed to occupations avoided by the Australian worker in a period of full employment, because of their nature and/or location. Many of the least desirable unskilled occupations were rural: canecutting typified the least desirable unskilled occupations to which the displaced persons were allocated.

1 L.W. Holborn, *The International Refugee Organization: A Specialized Agency of the United Nations. Its History and Work 1946-1952*, London 1956, p. 1.

2 See Appendix D.

The Australian sugar industry, like cane sugar industries the world over, was plagued by the difficulties of obtaining sufficient labour for the most unattractive field tasks. Cane sugar cultivation was for the most part repetitious, laborious and suited to gang methods. Various sources of labour were pursued over time in order to satisfy the enormous demands for labour characteristic of tropical crop agriculture in a pre-mechanized situation. While it was claimed that the white race could not labour in physically demanding occupations in the tropics, black, Asian and Southern European people were considered constitutionally suited to such labour. However, the heaviest of the canefield tasks, canecutting, tended to be avoided by white and black labour alike. Under those circumstances a servile, bonded workforce was thought to be the most practicable for canecutting. Hence, in Australia Asian and Melanesian indentured labour, and contract migrant white labour, were employed so long as cane was produced by manual labour. Common to these forms of canefield labour was migration and coercion. Displaced persons, like their predecessors in the industry, were coerced and bonded.

The Australian sugar industry was vulnerable to labour shortages in periods of full employment. By the late 1940s many field tasks had been mechanized but the most laborious, canecutting, remained a manual operation. The contracted displaced persons, transported to Australia in such large numbers, destined for rural and unskilled labour appeared a godsend to the sugar industry. Comparatively few displaced persons were coerced into 'volunteering' for canecutting in tropical North Queensland: perhaps no more than 2,000. Nevertheless, the industry lauded them as 'saviours' of the industry, coming to the rescue at a critical time of acute labour shortage.

Those migrants walked into an industry in transition, for already endeavours were in progress to mechanize cane harvesting and solve the perennial labour problems once and for all. The Northern area was faster to mechanize the various facets of cane cultivation than other areas.[3] However, the various regions of Australian cane sugar cultivation in the late 1940s and early 1950s differed not only in the degree of mechanization adopted but also in the manual methods employed to carry out the numerous field tasks. The cutters of northern districts between Mossman and Ingham, cut and loaded cane in somewhat different ways to their more southern counterparts. Climatic conditions and geographical aspects were of course the determinants of the methods utilized. Disconcertingly, different methods were used even within regions. What will be described below is one among several ways a cutter of the late 1940s and early 1950s might go about his work.

On arrival in Australia, the displaced person who cut cane adopted two new identities: that of a New Australian, and of a canecutter. The canecutter, living in relatively primitive conditions, labouring at back-breaking work, conjured in the popular imagination two apparently discrepant images: that of beast and that of hero. Poetry, prose, drama, cartoons and humour helped to perpetuate those images.

3 P.P. Courtenay (*et al.*), *The Settlement and Population Characteristics, Johnstone District, Queensland Sugar Coast*, Townsville 1974, p.13.

An examination of the canecutters' habitation, leisure activities, work routine, physical condition as a result of the demands of their labour, requisite skills, particular industrial reputation, and relationships with farmers and officials gives an insight into not just a means of employment but a unique and fascinating way of life. It was a way of life and work that many men relinquished eagerly, but in which others revelled. The latter sadly watched their skills become redundant, their life style outdated, their stature diminished. With the demise of the canecutter the character of sugar towns changed forever.

Displaced persons offered a unique experience to the small communities into which they were introduced. They were of many nationalities: amongst them Estonians, Lithuanians, Latvians, Ukrainians, Poles, Czechs, Yugoslavs and Russians. Most of the sugar towns had never received people of those nationalities before. Many had been tradesmen, professionals and students. It was characteristic of these migrants that their migration was permanent. A good proportion felt that they would not and could not ever return home. They were irrevocably estranged from family and birth place. War had changed their lives in a way none had anticipated or desired. Migration was not a choice of destinies but the only course available. Australia, in many cases, was not an eagerly awaited and anticipated new homeland but one of a number of alternative destinations that presented itself first, or most easily. For those men, adaptation to canecutting was not simply a matter of adjusting their bodies to the demands of a very strenuous labour. They were compelled, simultaneously, to conform to the expectations and mores of a different society: to learn a new language, to overcome homesickness and the trauma of estrangement, to lower their expectations of life goals, to endure loneliness, prejudice and occasionally exploitation, to live in locations and residences that were alien and unpleasant.

Studying those men as canecutters reinforced a picture of ordinary men: largely grateful for work; working hard to accrue some monetary security; aspiring to more skilled and satisfying work when the opportunity presented; no more conforming to the beast or hero characterization than the average Australian canecutter.

This study of the displaced person as canecutter is unique for two reasons. Firstly the employ of canecutting and the canecutting lifestyle has never before been described in such detail. Secondly, the role of the displaced person as labour in one particular post-war industry has never previously been highlighted. The writer recognizes that this study is in no way definitive. It is acknowledged that the small number of interviewees may not be a representative sample.

The Australian sugar industry viewed favourably the contribution these men made. Their work output and ethics, their adaptability and their demeanour were lauded. Though their benefit to the industry was great, the original number of these men was comparatively small. Some have died; others left the sugar districts for southern centres after a few weeks or months of cutting, having found the labour too difficult. Others moved away after honourably fulfilling their contracts. They were political refugees: of those who were accessible a substantial number still live with fear and suspicion and refuse to share their experiences. Those interviewed were accessible, and willing to divulge often intimate personal experiences. They were generous with their time, trusting in lending their photographs and magnanimous in sharing of their memories. This study is indebted to those "Gentlemen of the Flashing Blade"[4] not only for factual material but for the inspiration to be found in their life experiences; their fulfilled and thwarted dreams; their attitudes and courage.

I draw heavily on *The Cruel Field* and other works written by this author who cut cane during the 1950s. While he cut cane in the season, he wrote during the slack. He described the life and work realistically and skilfully without embroidery or sensationalism. For those who love the North Queensland sugar country and remember the cane cutting days, his writing has a poignant vividness, a memory-stirring quality that is unparalleled. It will be said that one of those "Gentlemen of the Flashing Blade", a Branko Domanovic, arrived on the I.R.O. ship, the *Mohammedi*, that in May 1949 he volunteered to cut cane and as one of a gang of nine men detrained in Ingham late in the same month. His name will not be found on the passenger list of that ship, nor was a pay ever drawn up for a displaced person canecutter of his name. In name, Branko Domanovicé never existed; yet he is every displaced person who migrated to Australia. Horror and upheaval, loss and fear, survival and hope: these are the ingredients in varying proportions of all displaced persons stories. Branko Domanovic is the sum of those; the exponent of a tale.[5]

After the Second World War displaced person canecutters made an inestimable contribution to the North Queensland sugar industry, North Queensland society and North Queensland history. It is a contribution that is long overdue for recognition.

4 J. Naish, *The Cruel Field*, London 1962, p.114.

5 However, I am especially indebted to the recollections of those interviewees who did arrive in Australia on board the *Mohammedi*, particularly those of Ukranian canecutter and canefarmer: F.N., and Yugoslav canecutter: V.V. It must be noted that Branko's story in no way resembles the story of either man's life.

CHAPTER 1

The "Adventure of Conquest"[1] begins

I see the bewildered migrants unshipped, untrained, debussed, debilleted, despatched to conquer the bush. The enemies await: the heat, the bad cuts and bad breaks; isolation in vastness and finally the slack.[2]

1 P. Bosi, *Farewell Australia*, Sydney 1972, p.29.
2 J. Naish, *That Men Should Fear*, London 1963, p.255.

Willie's booted foot lay disconcertingly close to Branko's right ear, its sole a tale of toil and impatience. Branko twitched his rolled coat sideways a few inches, its coarse texture irritating his neck in the wintery warmth. Nevertheless it made a satisfactory pillow as he lay under the fanning foliage of a giant raintree. Myriad shapes of blue, light and shadow dappled the ground where the new arrivals sprawled awaiting yet another formality: the sign-on. The reclining figures wore resignation. For these displaced people in quest of peace, safety and security the years since the end of the war had been milestoned by interviews, forms, contracts, and scrawled signatures.

Ingham watched the progress of the new migrants from the railway station to the main street with some curiosity and a little scepticism. The curiosity, however, was tempered for the detraining in 1948 of displaced persons headed for the canefields of the Ingham district had introduced the community to their foreign ways and languages.[3]

The farmers were already acquainted with their gangs, for rough introductions had been exchanged at the railway station before they loaded the weary and hungry men on to trucks and buses. Now they came across to the huddle and sprawl of bodies to lead them out from the shadow of the raintrees into the sunshine of the sign-on. The formality was being conducted on the verandah of the Cane Growers' Office building especially to sign on the newly arrived displaced persons gangs. They had arrived in time for the beginning of the season. It was Wednesday, the first day of June 1949 and the harvest was set to begin at dawn on the sixth of June.

After being issued with a union ticket and signing their season's contract to cut cane Branko and his friends were shown across the road to an Italian eating house. Ravenously consuming crumbed steak and copious servings of spaghetti they were lulled temporarily into a sense of well-being and convivial optimism.[4] Back on board the tray of the truck they slumbered in the hazy sunshine whilst the ganger and cook were shown into a store to place a food order. Jostled against baggage and bodies they were transported out of town along a cane-rimmed road that stretched on and on inexorably till finally a narrow farm track led them into silence and isolation.

The first inspection of the barracks, overgrown with grass; the encounter with the carpet snake coiled fearlessly in the out-house; the first night's fitful repose on sagging stretchers; the thorough sweeping-out of the generous littering of rat droppings and down of dust - all became by Saturday amusing anecdotes in letters home. Sunday

3 Ingham was already cosmopolitan, its inhabitants including Finnish, Spanish, Basque and Italian, but few if any of the nationalities represented amongst DPs were living there.

4 Arrangements for the migrants' reception varied at the different sugar towns. Usually they were met by the farmer in whose barracks they were to reside. In Ingham in 1948, and again in 1949, the gangs were met at the railway station by the A.W.U. Organizer, the Cane Growers' Secretary and the C.E.S. Employment Officer. They were introduced to the farmers to whom they would be contracted by the Cane Growers' Secretary. They were then taken to the Cane Growers' Office building. Afterwards they could be taken to a clothing store to buy work clothes and then to a grocery store to buy a stock of food, the cost of which was met from the first pay. Then they went to a cafe for a meal, similarly the cost of which also came from their first pay. Yugoslav canecutter and canefarmer M.M., interviewed 21 October 1984. Others were taken to a hotel where the farmer and licencee shouted them drinks. Some purchased their bread and stores at a small country shop along the route to the farm.

evening saw them returning to the barracks, grubby and relieved from their first burn. All over the district sproutings of ruddy fire-glow and grey smudges of smoke heralded the new season.

The eve of his initiation into the labour of canecutting Branko spent more awake than asleep, choked by smothering darkness, frightened and disturbed by the eerie cries of the curlews and the husky coughs and thunderous skatings of the possums. The pathetic, unfortunate and whimsical events that had led him to this spot 'under the Australian sky'[5] forced themselves on him uninvited for his reluctant contemplation. As he finally fell into uneasy sleep he was home again safe and loved, his lips on the warm, plump, rosy cheek of his aunt; an eager friend hopping from one impatient foot to another at the wooden gate waiting for him to set off on their ramble.

5 L. Markovic, *Ispod Australskog Neba* (*Under the Australian Sky*), Zagreb 1973. The author lived and worked in Australia before the War, and cut cane in North Queensland.

CHAPTER 2

Displaced Persons

Pea soup had become distasteful to the refugees in Lindau camp, and their sweet illusions had become bitter. Their minds were now obsessed with the idea of escaping somewhere far from Europe. They began making plans to go to Venezuela or Argentina or elsewhere... At the time of the deepest desperation, the Camp Office announced that Australia would take displaced persons.... Next day Opal called on Stan, and together they walked to the hut where the clever Poles could adjust anybody to the requirements of the Australian Minister for Immigration, Mr. Calwell.[1]

1 V.L. Borin, *The Uprooted Survive*, London 1959, pp.112, 126.

Orphaned at birth Branko Domanovic was reared by his mother's brother, a store-keeper and his kindly, gentle wife. They lived in a relatively prosperous town in North Bosnia, a scenicly splendid and varied region of Yugoslavia. In 1941 when Bosnia was occupied by the Axis forces, he was 17 years of age, had just graduated from a technical school and was uncertain about his future. Branko was lucky: his uncle certainly was not wealthy but was comfortable enough to be able to indulge his nephew upon whom he and his wife doted. Where Branko's life had been regulated by the gentle and predictable rhythm of a happy family life, study and friendship with other youngsters who enjoyed vigorous walks and rowing on the plentiful waterways of their region, it was now to be torn asunder.

In Bosnia, now incorporated into the so-called 'Independent State of Croatia', manipulation of regional animosities by the occupying forces resulted in the slaughter and forcible removal of many of its peoples. Again Branko Domanovic was luckier than most. He was to survive, but at the cost of family and homeland. While hiding with friends in a nearby city, he and other men were rounded up and transported by the Germans to the north of Germany where he was to embark on a remarkable adventure.

Though sent to work in a munitions factory he did not remain there long. Boyish recklessness and a sense of adventure undampened, he found his way across Germany to Vienna by wit and subterfuge. There he secured work with a construction company, finally moving on to Graz when the war ended. There he located his aunt's cousin into whose home he was warmly welcomed. He shared a room with the son of the house and was able to secure a job at the foundry where this young man worked.

During his time in Graz Branko befriended others uprooted like himself and even more alone. Bereft of family and home, fearful of returning to a country that had undergone catastrophic changes, political, social or geographical, convinced that Europe would continue to be politically unstable, these refugees and displaced persons looked to resettlement in lands far distant where perhaps they could start life anew. The International Refugee Organization (I.R.O.) offered them hope.[2]

As early as 1944 the United States together with 43 other countries had created the United Nations Relief and Rehabilitation Administration (U.N.R.R.A.) to assist the already urgent problem of displaced persons. With the cessation of hostilities the Allied Military Authorities and the U.N.R.R.A. were faced with the task of repatriating those who would be repatriated and finding a solution for those unwilling or unable to return home. This task, however, was only one of U.N.R.R.A.'s activities. Consequently, on 12 February 1946, the General Assembly of the United Nations, recognised the need for a specialized agency to deal exclusively with the problem, and established the International Refugee Organization (I.R.O.). Since it was hoped that displaced persons would be repatriated or resettled quickly the I.R.O.'s mandate lasted only from 1 July 1947 to 31 December 1951.[3]

2 International Labour Office, International Migration 1945-1957, Geneva 1959, p.46

3 *Ibid.*

Most displaced persons resettled by the I.R.O. "were Eastern European being predominantly Yugoslavs, Poles, Ukrainians, Czechs, Rumanians, Hungarians and people from the Baltic states."[4] The I.R.O. offered these varied people the prospect of a new home and a better life far away from war-torn Europe. The poignant reality was that though, in the circumstances, most wished to go as far away as possible from their homelands, if the choice had been theirs they would never have left Europe after the war; they would have returned home.[5] A common dream of new arrivals in Australia was "when they made good money and their country was free they would go home."[6]

Others though a little saddened by the finality of their departure were well pleased to be leaving Europe and their homelands behind them. Frequently those who had lived in poverty at home before the war and who could look forward to no improvement if they returned home were indifferent to the permanency of their departure. Similiarly those who had lost family in the war or whose family situation and relationships before the war had been unsatisfactory felt little regret. In those cases immigration may have been attractive whether the war had intervened or not, though it might have been an unattainable dream. A Polish immigrant who had known only poverty in Poland

> ... would not have had any opportunity to leave Poland. It was impossible to do that. A person could only do that if they were rich. If they were poor there was no way they could leave. During the war he saw Poland; before the war he had only seen an 100 square km. area around his village.[7]

Those like Branko whose families had been well-to-do, who had known economic and familial security, who had sound career prospects were the ones who most regretted the upheavals of war and the political revolutions their countries had undergone. But for those cataclysmic changes they would never have left home.[8]

Branko's desire to return home to discover the fate of his uncle and aunt was firmly outweighed by the conviction that he did not wish to experience life under a communist regime temporarily or permanently. He did know that he wanted to go to a place where he could breathe freely and move without looking over his shoulder. To Branko

4 For a succinct and well-written account of the origins of the displaced persons, see L.W. Holborn, *The International Refugee Organisation*, London 1965.

5 Lithuanian canecutter G.Z., interviewed 31 October 1984.

6 *Ibid.*

7 Polish canecutter K.M., interviewed 9 November 1984.

8 Yugoslav canecutter and canefarmer M.M., interviewed 21 October 1984 and Polish canecutter A.S., interviewed 8 November 1984.

Australia sounded like that place. Its distance from Europe,[9] its size, small population,[10] flexible social structure[11] and youthful image attracted him equally.

Australia was by no means the first choice of destination of other prospective immigrants he was to meet; for most, it was not even on their short list. The U.S.A., Canada and South America were the most common first choices. In many cases Australia was chosen only after they learned that quotas for the other destinations were tight or the waiting period a matter of years rather than months.[12] Some immigrants had the idea that in order to eventually reach the U.S.A., Australia could be used as a stepping stone rather than waiting out the time interminably in displaced persons' camps in Europe.[13] Certainly, research conducted in the early 1950s revealed that though:

> A few had preferred Australia for its remoteness from troubled Europe, or in the belief that economic opportunities were greater in an undeveloped country.... For many, Australia was the best available alternative to a refugee camp in Europe; for a few, the isolation of the Antipodes was a means of escape from unhappy memories.[14]

Usually the destination was decided by circumstances; where choice was possible it was often made for slight and arbitrary reasons. One migrant's wife wanted them to migrate to Brazil because there would be plenty of coffee available to them to drink there.[15] Another was inspired to migrate to North Queensland after reading a Joseph Conrad novel set in the Coral Sea;[16]; yet another decided not to migrate to Argentina on hearing that migrants to that country had to work their land grants with *bulls*.[17] In one apt description the displaced persons' migration from Europe was compared to that "... of a bird in the fog."[18] Sadly, while many migrants perceived resettlement as a temporary measure to be endured until they could return home,[19] most never did. Not without reason they came to feel that they had nothing to return to. However some who had found in Australia something of their 'eldorado' made sentimental and

9 Yugoslav canecutter M.L., interviewed 15 May 1983, and Yugoslav canecutter J.P., interviewed 31 March 1984.

10 Yugoslav canecutter D.N., interviewed 28 May 1983, and Yugoslav canecutter G.M. Questionnaire completed 12 November 1984.

11 Yugoslav canecutter V.V. Questionnaire completed early 1983.

12 Yugoslav canecutter and canefarmer M.M., interviewed 21 October 1984. One migrant claimed that in fact the quickest way to get out of Europe was to go to Australia. Czech canecutter R.C., interviewed 8 March 1985.

13 *Ibid.*, and Polish canecutter A.S., interviewed 8 November 1984.

14 A. Sherington, *Australia's Immigrants 1788-1978*, Sydney 1980, p.136. See also L. Martin, *Refugee Settlers*, Canberra 1965, p.50.

15 Russian canecutter B.I., interviewed 7 November 1984.

16 Polish canecutter A.S., interviewed 8 November 1984.

17 Yugoslav canecutter M.L., interviewed 15 May 1983.

18 Yugoslav canecutter D.N., interviewed 28 May 1983.

19 Martin, *op. cit.*, p.50.

anxious holiday journeys home renewing acquaintance with relatives 'lost' to them for over three decades. Others still dream that the old man will go home one day.[20]

That displaced person migrants were able to be resettled so promptly in Australia was due in great part to the vision and energy of one man, Arthur A. Calwell. Less than a month after becoming Minister for Immigration he announced the Government's immigration policy to the House of Representatives.[21] The Australian Population and Immigration Council in its 1977 study expressed most succinctly the concerns which the policy embodied:

> the fear of foreign invasion during World War II gave rise to the belief in the immediate post war period that Australia needed to increase significantly its population. Coupled with this belief was the urge to develop and reconstruct the economy rapidly. Industrial development in Australia during the war had highlighted the possibilities for industrial expansion. Sufficient numbers of persons with the necessary skills, however, were not available, or likely to be available, from natural increase alone.[22] It could be argued that this is an oversimplification. The population debate had been going on long before the Second World War. The population/defence concern had been debated even before the Pearl Harbour bombing. It has been argued that the post-war defence argument was encouraged in order to win public support for a potentially unpopular large-scale immigration scheme.[23]

It was calculated that the immigrant intake would need to be 70,000 per annum or 1 per cent of a population of 7 million with a 1 per cent natural increase.[24]

In September 1945 the Australian Delegation to the International Labour Conference held in Paris had toured Europe in its additional role of an Immigration Advisory Committee to ascertain the possibilities for European migration to Australia.[25] Its report recommended that migrants from Europe as well as Britain be sought, but as the committee had not toured refugee camps it did not mention displaced persons.

As the United Kingdom was considered the most desirable source of immigrants resumption of an Assisted Passages scheme of migration for British immigrants was

20 The saying "Go west young man, go home old man" readily comes to mind in relation to the displaced person migrant and his trips home. (Source unknown).

21 A.A. Calwell, *Immigration, Policy and Progress*, Canberra 1949, p.68.

22 Australian Population and Immigration Council, *Immigration Policies and Australia's Population*, Canberra 1977, pp.24-25.

23 E.F. Kunz "The Genesis of the Post-War Immigration Programme and the Evolution of the Tied-Labour Displaced Persons Scheme", *Ethnic Studies*, No. 1 (1977), pp.30-31.

24 Kunz, *op. cit.* p.34. See also. W.D. Borrie, "Economic and Demographic Aspects of Post-War Immigration to Australia", *R.E.M.P. Bulletin*, 3, No. 1 (1955), p.3. Intake increased to nearly two per cent per annum in 1949 and 1950.

25 *Ibid.*, p.35.

planned.[26] By 1947 free and assisted passage schemes from Britain to Australia were in operation.[27] However, there were obstacles to attracting British migrants or those from other favoured sources such as western and northern Europe; one, major and continuing, was lack of shipping. Many intending to migrate became tired of waiting and found their chance in the reburgeoning home economies.[28]

The Government was already committed to admitting 8000 refugees on humanitarian grounds. Apart from these, Calwell in early 1947 stated unequivocally that applications by intending European migrants including refugees

> would be more selective from the point of view of the intending migrants' ability to contribute to Australia's *economic* welfare, with particular regard to their ages and proficiency in those skilled occupations where there was a marked shortage of labour.[29]

Those granted landing permits would have been nominated by a relative or friend in Australia who had pledged to house and maintain them. This policy would remain in force until the U.N. had devised means to solve the displaced persons problem conclusively. He emphasised that the Government would continue to give precedence to British immigrants. It was his avowed vision that:

> ... few ... these victims of man's inhumanity will be when set against the scores of thousands - and ultimately the hundreds of thousands - of our own kith and kin whom we propose to bring from the United Kingdom to these shores...[30]

Nevertheless on 21 July 1947 an agreement was signed with the I.R.O. for admission of displaced persons from Europe;[31] the first group arrived in Fremantle on the *General Heintzelman* on 28 November 1947. Under the agreement 4000 displaced persons were to be admitted in 1947 and 12,000 a year thereafter.[32] In justification Calwell said that Australia, being a full member of and a financial contributor to the I.R.O. had therefore "a definite responsibility for contributing to the solution of the displaced persons problem ..."[33]

Approximately 170,000 displaced persons arrived in Australia under the scheme. The greater proportion were Poles and people from the Baltic States. People of

26 E. Jaggard, "Australian Immigration 1900-1950: a survey", *Historicus* 7 (1973), p.17.

27 Calwell, *op. cit.*, pp.68-69.

28 Kunz, *op. cit.*, p.35.

29 Statement to the House of Representatives, 1 January 1948, p.7. AA: CRS A432, 1939-1947; 47/287.

30 *Ibid.*, p.11.

31 F Kunz, "European Migrant Absorption in Australia"; *International Migration* 9, (1971), 1 & 2, p.70.

32 "Clearly 12,000 D.P.'s within the target of 70,000 annual total went beyond the one-10 non-British ratio mentioned in [Calwell's] first ministerial statement". Kunz, *op. cit.*, p.37.

33 Financial membership did not oblige a nation to accept refugees. Calwell, *op. cit.*, p.53.

Russian, Ukrainian and Yugoslav, Czech and Hungarian nationality also arrived in considerable numbers.[34] The attractions of this migration were multifarious. The I.R.O. provided the shipping. Migrants could be selected using well-nigh any criteria, conditions and restrictions the Australian Government wished to exercise.[35]

A scarcity of shipping restricted the British Scheme to perhaps 12,000 or 15,000 immigrants per annum. So by mid-1948 the prospect of immediate non-British migration was enthusiastically invited with Australia being prepared "to take as many of these fine settlers as shipping can be provided for ..."[36] Ultimately they were to exceed assisted and unassisted British migration substantially.[37]

Though shipping the displaced persons from Europe to Australia was the I.R.O.'s responsibility, Australia undertook to make an *ex gratia* payment of £10 sterling for each adult migrant brought out under the I.R.O. auspices to compensate for the distance they had to be shipped. In addition the Australian Government recruited and selected its migrants, conducted medical examinations, catered for their reception on arrival, placed them in employment and arranged for the housing of dependants until suitable accommodation with the family head could be found.[38] An interesting feature of post World War II immigration, and particularly of the Displaced Persons Scheme was the extent of government planning and administration. Because of the scale and nature of the displaced person migration the Commonwealth Government rather than the State Governments took on those responsibilities.

The policy which evolved as a result of Australia's involvement with the I.R.O. was formulated in terms of Government priorities, particularly economic development. Indeed the whole scheme was conditional on its being of economic benefit to the nation. In the Australian Delegation's statement to the U.N. Economic and Social Council Special Committee on Refugees and Displaced Persons it was stipulated that:

> The Australian Government will not, however, initiate any large scale plan of immigration unless it is possible, within reasonable limits, to ensure the economic future of intending migrants, and to meet the obligations to our community ...[39]

34 See Appendix A, Table 1.

35 Kunz, "Genesis of the Post-War Immigration Programme", p.30.

36 Conference of Commonwealth and State Ministers on Immigration - Agenda Item 13, p.25, "Displaced Persons Scheme". AA: CRS A445, 1948-; 145/3/4.

37 See Appendix A, Table 2.

38 Notes for Interdepartmental Conference to be held 18th May 1950. "Problems of migration of skilled tradesmen to Australia, (c) Displaced Persons Resettlement Scheme", p.2. AA: CRS A445, 1951-1955; 179/1/6.

39 Australian Statement on Resettlement of Refugees in Australia". I.R.O. Australian Delegation Reports; Annexe D, p.14. AA: CRS A1838, 1949-; 861/5/2.

In his book, *Arrivals and Departures,* Jupp observed that to ensure that the displaced persons fulfilled both their obligations to the community and their anticipated role of cultivating or developing the nation's resources Australia, which had formerly "fought against indentured labour, was quite happy to impose two years of bonded employment in manual work as its price for humanitarianism."[40] Every displaced person between the ages of 16 and 50 who migrated to Australia independently, or under the I.R.O. Scheme, was admitted 'under exemption' and was required, upon selection, to sign a form of 'Undertaking'[41] to remain for two years from the date of arrival in whatever occupation and locality was determined for them by the Commonwealth Employment Service, The Immigration Department's agent for placing migrants in employment.[42] As the second party to this 'Undertaking' was the Commonwealth the displaced person could be reallocated to another employer or locality if for any reason the placement proved unsatisfactory. Disciplinary action could be taken against a displaced person who "openly and flagrantly disregarded his obligation".[43] At the worst that could be deportation. Migrants who fulfilled their obligations were formally permitted to remain permanently at the end of the specified two years; their change of status was signified by the receipt of a 'Certificate of Authority to Remain in Australia'. Thence forward they could seek the help of the Commonwealth Employment Service to obtain employment but were not bound to remain in the employment found for them, nor in any particular locality.[44]

According to Kunz the policy of requiring displaced persons to "enter into such open-ended indentures as a pre-condition of their settlement"[45] was pursued by few countries; Australia was the only major recipient country to make such an 'Undertaking' basic to its admission policy. Selection "with a view to meeting ... known labour requirements" primarily unskilled, "obviated the necessity of matching [skills] with vacancies and was a key factor in enabling Australia to become the recipient of more D.P.'s than any other country except the U.S.A."[46]

The 'indenture system' then, assured that the large intake of displaced persons could be controlled and directed to filling labour shortfalls in heavy industry, public utilities, rural areas and domestic hospital employ: as Borrie put it, "the donkey work ... which ... Australians were only too willing to avoid".[47] One unskilled occupation to which displaced persons were directed was canecutting. The third I.R.O. transport to Australia the *General Black* carried the first displaced persons destined for the sugar fields of New South Wales and Queensland.

40 J. Jupp, *Arrivals and Departures*, Melbourne 1966, p.8.

41 Appendices C & D.

42 "Notes for Mr. W. McMahon, M.P. on Two Year Contracts for Migrants", p.1. AA: CRS A445, 1951-1955; 179/9/5 Pt 3.

43 "Displaced Person Migrant Workers absconding from Direct Employment - Deportation". Memo. 18 Sept. 1950 by A.L. Nutt, Acting Secretary Dept. of Labour & Nat. Service. AA: CRS A445, 1951-1955; 179/9/5 Pt 3.

44 See appendix G.

45 Kunz, *op. cit.*, p.38.

46 *Ibid.*

47 W.D. Borrie, "Australia's New Population Pattern", in H.Holt (et al.), *Australia and the Migrant*, Sydney 1953, p.42.

That labour had to be imported into the sugar fields under coercion was not new or unusual. The use of imported non-white labour was almost universal in cane sugar cultivation. Even where the industry operated under free and competitive conditions its seasonal character and the unattractive nature of field tasks made it difficult to attract and hold labour. Historically white labour was generally unavailable, or where available, unreliable. Belief prevailed that the white person, even if willing, was physically incapable of executing even the simplest of out-doors work in the tropics. Southern Europeans were seen as an exception; "people of southern European stock may have some competitive advantage over people of north-western European origin because of greater adaptability to tropical climates".[48]

North Queensland's first southern European community comprised Italians who came to work as canecutters on the canefields in the late 1800s, and who had been indentured for two years. Italians were continuing to migrate to the North Queensland canefields in large numbers even in the 1950s. It has been suggested that the spectacular growth of the sugar industry in Queensland in the first half of this century was very much related to this great migration of Italians.[49] Other southern Europeans who commonly migrated to Queensland were Spanish, Maltese and Yugoslav. The migration of such peoples whether permanent or transitory was indubitably critical to the viability of the North Queensland sugar industry at various times, including the post war period.

In 1947 quite a number of Queensland sugar districts were suffering an acute labour shortage, expected to be even more acute with a projected heavier crop in the 1948 season. It seemed that "the best prospects of immediate relief are through the endeavours to obtain for use in the Sugar Industry some of the 'displaced persons'....." who it was thought, would be suitable for canecutting because Australia was especially selecting men between 18 and 35 years who would be suited to hard work. The fact that they would be entering Australia under a 'certificate of exemption' guaranteed that those selected for canecutting could be retained for at least one season. In addition they could be directed to the sugar districts where the need was greatest.[50] The

48 J.L.T. Wilson, "Northmost Queensland", *Current Affairs Bulletin* 12 No.12, Sept.1953, p.191.

49 J.P. Hempel, *Italians in Queensland: Some Aspects of the Postwar Settlement of Italian Migrants*, Canberra 1959, p.167.

50 Letter 16 October 1947, E.T.S. Pearce Gen. Sec. Aust. Sugar Producers Assoc. AA: CRS A445, 1947-1951; 179/1/3 pt 3.

attraction of migrant labour under contract was irresistible. "Not to try those Balts as canecutters would rather be looking a gift horse in the mouth".[51]

At the peak of their optimism cane industry officials proposed that the Commonwealth Government assign for the 1948 season between "2,500 and 2,800 and this number does not allow fully for replacement".[52] Nowhere near that number would be allocated but the Chairman of the Commonwealth Immigration Advisory Council, Leslie Haylen reported that:

> After hearing all the evidence put before it the Council was satisfied that there was an acute and dangerous shortage of labour in the Australian sugar industry. It therefore decided to recommend to you:-
>
> (a) that the Department should endeavour to fulfill the labour requirements of the sugar industry by allotting 1,000 migrants arriving under I.R.O. or other auspices.[53]

The Immigration Department agreed to carry out both recommendations.[54] On 5 November 1948 there were 818 displaced persons working in the sugar fields of Queensland.[55] By 14 October 1949, the year Branko started canecutting, the number had risen to 909.[56]

51 *Ibid.*, p.2. In Australia displaced person migrants were variously referred to as Balts (properly people from the former Baltic states of Latvia, Lithuania and Estonia), D.P.'s (displaced persons), or Reffos (refugees), terms not always used kindly. See C.J. Burrows & C. Morton, *The Canecutters*, Melbourne 1986, pp.110, 121.

52 R. Muir, Gen. Sec. Q Canegrowers Council & E. Pearce, Aust Sugar Producers Assoc. to Calwell 11 Dec 1947. AA: CRS A445, 1947-1951: 179/1/3 pt 3 p.1.

53 L. Haylen, Chmn. C'th. Immigration Advisory Coun., to Calwell 23 Feb 1948. *Ibid.*

54 *Ibid.*

55 "Statement of Placement of Displaced Persons by Industries as at 5/11/1948." AA: CRS A434, 1939-1950; 50/3/13/ pt 2.

56 Weekly Statement by Industries of Displaced Persons Employed in Australia. AA: CRS 574/1, 1940-1950; 573/2/23 pt 1.

CHAPTER 3

From Europe to the Queensland Cane Fields

A long procession marched to the railway station in Bagnolia, taking the train to Naples, the port of embarkation for Australia. There was absolute silence among the crowds on the decks. Their minds were far away - on the shores of the Baltic Sea, on the green plains of Poland, on the dark soil of the Ukrainian steppes, in the Carpathian Highlands, on the Hungarian Pustzta, in the Bohemian Hills - in countries where all the people they knew, people speaking their language, still lived... Yes in Europe were their motherlands ...[1]

1 Borin, *The Uprooted Survive*, p.134.

Branko, encouraged by tales from other displaced persons who had gone to the I.R.O. Head Office in Graz to register for resettlement, decided to try his luck. Prospective migrants underwent stringent medical and psychological examinations carried out by both the I.R.O. officials and the selection teams of the various recipient countries. Though official material spoke of displaced persons being put through up to five medical examinations[2] prior to embarkation, many probably only had to endure three at the most. A medical examination might include a test of agility for which the prospective migrant had to jump on and off a table.[3] The psychologist's examination could be fairly stringent. While being scrutinized for signs of mental instability,[4] their given motives for migration were also being minutely investigated. Persons with political or criminal records were supposed to be rejected.[5] Though they were being selected in the main as unskilled labour they were tested for literacy.[6] One overzealous interviewer was even known to enquire of prospective immigrants who had registered a desire to work in rural employment:

> ... about land; ... about cattle ... about growing grain like wheat .... They even asked about the piggery ... how long it takes the mother to have the young things; how long it takes the cow to have the calf ...[7]

After initial screening and documentation Branko was interviewed by an Australian Government Representative and underwent the various eligibility tests including medical and literacy. As a 'free-living' displaced person he continued to live with his relatives and work at the foundry. A couple of months passed before he received a letter informing him that his application for resettlement had been accepted and that he was to report to the I.R.O. Staging Centre or Assembly Camp at Trofaiach near Leoben. Suffering bitterly from the cold and fed little better than cabbage soup he was relieved to be transferred to the I.R.O. Embarkation Centre at Bagnoli in Italy after only three weeks. Not all migrants were so lucky. Time spent in camps waiting on selection for resettlement and consequently for a passage on a boat could exceed three years.

At Bagnoli Branko found the climate a little warmer and life more pleasant. He was able to go on a tour of Pompeii, see films at the Picture Theatre and indulge in a little black marketeering to pass time and make a bit of pocketmoney! During his three weeks there he underwent final scrutiny and a medical check. Finally in mid April 1949 he read with joyous anticipation his name on the roll posted on the camp notice board for the I.R.O. ship, the *Mohammedi*, setting sail from Naples for Melbourne, Australia.

On 11 April 1949, as the passengers of the *Mohammedi* lined its decks watching with amusement the mischievous antics of the homeless waifs on the wharf, they heard

2 See Appendix 3.

3 Yugoslav canecutter T.A., interviewed 14 May 1983.

4 Yugoslav canecutter and canefarmer M.M., interviewed 21 October 1984.

5 *Ibid.* Also Czech canecutter R.C., interviewed 8 March 1985. He underwent detailed questioning on his political history.

6 *Ibid.*

7 Ukrainian canecutter and canefarmer F.N., interviewed 3 November 1984.

from a distance the faint strains of an orchestra. Drawing level, a striking white ship docked stern to bow with the *Mohammedi*; it was the *New Hellas*, and the melody, 'Red River Valley'. As the music faded the charmed hush was broken by the bustle of disembarkation and the consequent embarkation of the displaced person passengers destined for Canada. In later years Branko was to always recall that afternoon with sadness. He still could conjure the faces of friends he had made in Bagnoli standing on the deck of the *New Hellas*, where the orchestra had played 'Red River Valley', extending their hands in gestures of endearment and farewell as the *Mohammedi* sailed away.

Though night shrouded sky and sea Branko stood late on the deck deep in reverie. As he took his last look at the fiery spate of Etna etched on the evening sky he came to terms with the fact that he would never see those friends again. The lost warm friendships were now as intangible as the strains of that never-to-be-forgotten melody.

Nevertheless that poignant leave-taking was coupled with a certain sense of relief. His sentiments were not unlike that of a fellow passenger on the *Mohammedi* who departed with

> very mixed feelings. Firstly he thought it was a relief to be finally on the way as during their six weeks in camp there were many rumours of departure which did not come true.... Realized the enormity of the step he had taken, what he was leaving behind: all his friends, his girlfriend, the life he had been used to. Thirdly, it was apprehension. What it would be like in the new land, what will happen if it does not work out as most of bridges were burnt, also a certain amount of dreaming and hoping especially when he reflected on the years from 1944-1949: what had happened, the drifting, the disappointments and most of all lack of future.[8]

Branko felt that it was an unkind fate to be a passenger on the *Mohammedi* after glimpsing the relative luxury of the *New Hellas*. The *Mohammedi* was manned by a seemingly lackadaisical Indian crew, and life on board was cramped, uncomfortable and tedious. Fed on a monotonous diet, bedded down in the converted holds, for three weeks they were left to their own devices. For single men like Branko card playing, conversing, wrestling and romantic trysts passed the time. So hot and stuffy were the sleeping quarters that most people slept on deck till rough weather and seasickness drove them below. Crossing of the Equator and the accompanying Neptunian rituals and pranks were a welcome diversion.

Understandably Branko viewed the first sight of the Australian shoreline with a considerable sense of relief. Especially for those who had suffered seasickness throughout the entire journey, reaching Australia was "like coming home to the Promised Land".[9] The boat docked in Melbourne late in the afternoon of 14 May. It was nightfall before they were disembarked and entrained. Like most migrants disembarking in Melbourne, passengers from the *Mohammedi* were taken to the Bonegilla Reception and Training Camp near Albury. The smell of hay, the long forlorn whistling of the train evoked for Branko images of the Wild West as the train made its

8 Yugoslav canecutter K.B., questionnaire completed early 1982.

9 Yugoslav canecutter G.M., questionnaire completed 12 November 1984.

way towards Albury. Though they arrived very late at Bonegilla a meal was waiting for them and after the *Mohammedi*'s fare it seemed a banquet.

Branko spent two week sat Bonegilla. Viewing his new country from the confines of that camp he was impressed by the parrots and their splendid plumage, the scant foliage of the gums, and the semi-wild nature of the land. Pino Bosi in *Farewell Australia* mirrored what Branko sensed:

> Light blue skies. Strange smells of gum-trees. Strange smells of sheep-meat. Dry grass, rolling hills, dead trees, parched land... I thought of Africa. Strange sense of adventure.[10]

Common pastimes at Bonegilla were hunting rabbits - a plentiful pest, or spending hours in circuitous political polemic.

Foremost of all the new migrants' concerns was to leave Bonegilla as soon as possible and secure a job. They discussed the possibilities amongst themselves and volunteered for any jobs available.[11] Most would have known that they had to remain for two years in whatever occupation they volunteered for or were directed to. Branko could remember signing a 'Form of Undertaking' in Europe and understood its ramifications; undoubtedly others did not recall[12] being informed by the Australian selection teams of the condition attached to their migration to Australia. As one expressed it: "The first time he realised he hadn't come for free was when he arrived at Bonegilla where the terms of the contract were spelt out".[13]

Branko and many of his acquaintances from Bonegilla were directed to rural employment. In the post War period of industrial recovery and expansion increased manpower requirements, particularly of the rural sector, could not be satisfied by available labour. It was envisaged that a substantial proportion of those immigrants who came out to Australia as displaced persons, would be directed to, and would hopefully remain in, the rural industries. It has been well documented, however, that this vision did not materialize. In fact a greater proportion of the migrants found their way if not immediately on arrival, at least as soon as their contracts expired, into the metropolitan areas where they found employment in manufacturing.[14] The Queensland sugar industry was foremost in requesting large numbers of displaced

10 Bosi, *Farewell Australia*, p.59.

11 Lithuanian canecutter G.Z., interviewed 31 October 1984.

12 Of the 16 interviewed four did not know of the two year contract; two acknowledged having signed the 'Form of Undertaking'; ten were aware of the two year contract but did not remember signing it.

13 Yugoslav canecutter and canefarmer M.M., interviewed 21 October 1984.

14 W.D. Borrie & J. Zubrzycki, "Employment of Post-War immigrants in Australia", *Int. Labour Rev.* 77 No 1, March 1973, p.248.

persons.[15] Nevertheless Queensland was to receive the least number of refugees: no more than 14,000 in all.[16] The state was at a disadvantage in attracting migrants. It was distant in their minds from the major urban centres, and from the reception centres in Victoria and New South Wales.[17] Instead of being shipped to ports close to the major areas - Cairns, Townsville or even Brisbane - they disembarked at Melbourne or Newcastle where it was comparatively easy to have their destination changed, or simply disappear into a bustling urban centre.[18]

Hempel argued that Queensland was unable to 'ingest' a great number of displaced persons anyway because of the comparatively undeveloped nature of its secondary industries and the limited number of industrial jobs offering. Instead, displaced persons were assigned to State and Local Authorities works such as road making and railway construction. This, he asserts "meant arduous work in remote places and did not encourage permanent settlement except, perhaps, in Brisbane".[19] Sugar was the only Queensland primary industry that absorbed and held any large numbers of migrants.[20]

Migrants, bound by their two-year contracts, were drafted into canecutting which most Australians disdained in the post war years of acute labour shortage.

Displaced persons were recruited for the sugar fields in either of two ways:

(a) some were specifically screened for suitability for sugar field work at the time of selection in Europe;[21]

(b) Some volunteered for canecutting labour while at the Reception Camps in Australia.

The first method did not necessarily destine migrants for the canefields, merely indicating their possible suitability. Labour priorities when they arrived in Australia, for the most part, determined their ultimate placement.

This prior 'screening' by officers ignorant of the real qualities desirous of a canecutter was a matter of grave concern to the Australian Sugar Producers' Association.

15 Muir and Pearce to Calwell, 11 Dec 1947 as above.

16 Stevens, "Immigration Policy for the Future", in Holt (et al.), *Australia and the Migrant*, p.142.

17 J.A. Hempel, "The Migration Problem in Queensland", *Ec. News*, 21 No 3, Mar 1952, p.1.

18 At various times over the years the question whether migrants could be landed at Queensland ports was asked of the Department of Immigration. The idea was always soundly quashed. Hansard: House of Representatives. Answers to Questions, Tuesday 30 May 1950. Also Department of Immigration, Senate Question, 13 July 1951. Question No. 2. Senator Wood to ask the Minister representing the minister for Immigration. Answer. AA: CRS A436, 1945-1950; 50/5/3482.

19 Hempel, op. cit., p.4.

20 *Ibid.*

21 G.V. Greenhalgh, Sen. Migration Officer to Sec. Dept. of Immigration 19 December 1947. AA: CRS A445 1947-1951, 179/1/3 pt 3. See also "Skilled Balts Resent Cutting Order", *Melbourne Age*, 28 April 1948; "Skilled Balts Sour over Sugar", *Courier-Mail*, 28 April 1948, cuttings in A434, 1939-50, 50/3/7188.

> Setting a standard of age and physique will not enable someone with no practical knowledge to select the right type of man. Experiences in this direction have proved a dismal failure. It is not only a question of size or the general physique of the man; there is a psychological aspect. Experience shows that much depends on the new cutter's determination to stick at the job and his mental approach to hard manual work.[22]

Though they requested that an officer with knowledge of the sugar industry be posted in Europe to carry out selections, the Government deemed this unnecessary.[23]

Instead a liaison officer was selected and sent down to Bonegilla on the arrival of a shipment of displaced persons from which selection for the sugar fields was to be made. He would help select men suitable to work as canecutters, and these would undergo a form of 'induction' course which apparently even included a film on canecutting.[24] though few remember viewing it. Before proceeding North they were grouped into gangs. They were encouraged to form these with 'mates' and to select one suitable member for cook.[25] If gangs were not composed of mates they were at least made up of men of their own nationality with whom they would naturally feel more at home.

The man chosen for the job of Liaison Officer was a Dan Callaghan,[26], strongly recommended for the position by both Muir and Pearce, General Secretaries of the Q.C.G.C. and A.S.P.A. respectively.

> Mr. Muir and myself have in mind an officer of the calibre of Mr. D. Callaghan who was closely associated with Sugar Industry Manpower Advisory Committee members during the war, and who has wide practical knowledge and appreciation of the Sugar Industry's harvesting labour requirements.[27]

22 E.T. Pearce, Secretary A.S.P.A. to President & Executive, 16 Oct 1947. AA: CRS 1947-1951; 179/1/3 pt 3.

23 R. Muir, Gen. Sec. Q.C.G.C. to T.H.E. Hayes, Dept. of Immigration, 9 Aug 1951. *Ibid.* 179/1/4 pt 4.

24 Ukrainian canecutter and canefarmer F.N., interviewed 3 November 1984.

25 E.T.S. Pearce, A.S.P.A. to Calwell December 1947. *Ibid.* 179/1/3 pt 3.

26 Normally employed in Brisbane as C.E.S. Rural Officer.

27 Pearce, letter of 16 Oct 1947; see above, fn.22.

Dan Callaghan was remembered well by ex-cutters for his rhetoric. Volunteers were not always 'fast in coming forward' for most seemed to want to stay in Sydney or Melbourne. It is recalled that Callaghan tried to inveigle recruits by painting a 'rosy picture' of canecutting, especially of its possible financial rewards. "You young fellows", he told them "will all be millionaires in 12 months!"[28]

As stated a migrant might have been informed at the time of selection that he could be directed to canecutting once in Australia but it was not general practice for Australian officials to make a prior designation to any occupation. The common experience was that a call for volunteers to cut cane was made at the Reception and Training Camps in Australia. Migrants volunteered for any number of reasons: because their friends did, or because they had heard of the job in Europe and thought they would like to try it,[29] or because of the promised monetary rewards:"everybody was young, greedy about the money".[30] Generally, they were ignorant of where in Australia cane grew, how it grew or what canecutting involved. Some envisaged it growing in water, like rice.[31]

It has not been possible to calculate the number of displaced persons inveigled into canecutting in the period 1948-1951.[32] Clearly it was substantial: according to an answer in the House of Representatives in 1948, "about 900 of them were sent to assist in harvesting the sugar crop", most of them between Ingham and Cairns.[33]

Again in 1949 at the height of the season 909 were at work,[34] a number of them for their second season. Of that number 350 left Brisbane by train on 30 May 1949:[35] amongst them Branko Domanovic and others who had arrived on the *Mohammedi* only a few weeks earlier.

There are no reliable figures available for the 1950 season though it is reasonable to assume that some displaced persons were allocated to the Queensland sugar industry in that year. In August 1951 T.H.E. Heyes, Secretary, Department of Immigration, wrote to R. Muir, General Secretary, Q.C.G.C. saying that it was "generally conceded that the displaced person played a significant part in the successful harvesting of the 1948, 1949 *and to a lesser extent the 1950 crop*.[36] Probably no more than 100 first time displaced persons were directed to the Queensland sugar fields for the 1951 harvest.[37]

28 Yugoslav canecutter and canefarmer M.M., interviewed 21 October 1984.

29 Polish canecutter A.S., interviewed 8 November 1984.

30 Ukrainian canecutter and canefarmer F.N., interviewed 3 November 1984.

31 Polish canecutter K.M., interviewed 9 November 1984.

32 Personal enquiries at the Commonwealth Archives in Brisbane, Sydney, Melbourne and Canberra, and at the State Archives and State Government Officer in Brisbane failed to elicit the necessary data. If it still exists it is probably in Melbourne among the records of the former Dept. of Labour and National Service, which clearance rules prevented me from examining in the time I had available.

33 Hansard, questions and answers in the H. of Representatives, 10 November 1948. AA: CRS A445, 1951-1955, 162/3/4.

34 Weekly Statement ... of Displaced Persons Employed in Australia. Sugar: Seasonal: Queensland: Males. Week ended 14 Oct. 1949. AA: CRS MP574/1, 1940-50; 573/2/23 pt.1.

35 "Manpower for 1949 Season: Displaced Persons for Canefields. *Aust. Sugar Journal*, 15 June 1949, p.209.

36 AA: CRS A445, 1951-1954; 179/1/4 pt.4. My emphasis.

37 Muir to H.E. Holt, Mins. for Labour etc. 30 May 1951. AA: CRS A445, 1947-1951; 179/1/3 pt.3.

Conflicting assertions and fragmentary figures baffle any attempt to deduce conclusively the numbers of displaced persons sent to North Queensland as canecutters: in all, perhaps 2000 between the years of 1948 and 1951.

In May 1949 when others were leaving Bonegilla for factories in Melbourne, Branko, always on the lookout for adventure, decided that canecutting was the job for him. The summoning of volunteers for canecutting reminded Branko of an 'army call-up', only in this case the enemy would be a strange and hardy plant; the battle ground, the wild unknown North; the dangers, such exotic primeval creatures as crocodiles and boa constrictors. His eager hopes were almost dashed when Yugoslav acquaintances forming a gang were initially reluctant to include him in their number feeling that his slender physique was not suitable. Finally Branko found himself one of a motley gang of nine, hardly more improbable canecutter material than others in the gang, namely the cobbler, musician and barber.

Before they were dispatched to their new occupations their basic requirements were provided for. Many had arrived destitute, with little clothing. On their arrival in Australia the Government had issued them with "heavy work boots, light shoes, socks, under clothing, shirt, sports coat and trousers or two piece suit, hat, tie" and other necessaries.[38] They also received a small monetary allowance which commenced with their arrival at the camp and ceased when they were in employment. In addition they were equipped with ration cards and most importantly, Alien Registration Cards which they were supposed to be able to produce whenever required. Those going to the canefields were sometimes issued with additional items: "two blankets, one pillow, two pairs of working trousers, one pair of sandshoes, and one mosquito net"[39] and in some cases two towels.[40] The cost would be deducted from their wages.

Much organization went into transporting the displaced persons from camps in the south to the cane fields in the north. Every care had to be taken that they did not become lost in transit for most did not speak English and had little idea of their exact destination. They travelled by train and the cost of their second class fare was met by the Department of Immigration. Arrangements were made for meals to be eaten at the various stations or in an attached dining car free of charge. As many as 40 gangs were transported at one time.

Late in the evening of 28th May 1949 one of those special trains pulled out of Albury station. Branko was a passenger. From his windowseat he leant out to gaze into the rushing night. Finally closing the window on the cold of a still foreign landscape he rested back against the unyielding seat to retrace in his memory all the train journeys he had made by force or choice since he was seventeen. In later years he could recollect only kaleidoscopic images of that last journey with destination 'unknown': blanket shrouded couples, a tableau in firelight, exchanging furtive last intimacies on the railway platform; a feast of chocolates that cost him all his pocket money; a cramped bus ride to the Hostel at Kangaroo Point; Pandanus palms mistaken for grotesquely monstrous pineapple plants.

38 Calwell to Pearce, A.S.P.A., December 1947. *Ibid.*

39 Heyes to Director, Bonegilla Centre, 12 May 1949. *Ibid.*

40 Heyes to Muir, 12 July 1949. *Ibid.*

In schedule, Branko's journey would have been somewhat similar to that taken by 355 displaced persons a year earlier. That special train left Albury at 8.50 p.m. on the 22nd May 1948. The next day passengers were given breakfast at Mossvale, lunch at Newcastle and tea at Gloucester. The breakfast stop on the 24th was made at Casino. All those stops were in N.S.W. When they arrived at the South Brisbane Station they were instructed:

> You will be taken (in two parties) to Kangaroo Point Hostel where provision has been made for you to have a hot bath, meals and rest.
>
> You will leave there at 6.45 p.m. and onward by bus, and entrain at Roma Street Station for destination.[41]

On the 25th they were given breakfast at Gladstone, lunch at Rockhampton and dinner at Mackay. On the 26th they breakfasted in Townsville and lunched at Cardwell. After Townsville, the first point of detraining, the gangs alighted at Ingham, Tully, Innisfail, Babinda, Gordonvale and finally Cairns, arriving there at 4.00 p.m. on the 26th May 1948.

Gangs of migrants destined for the canefields often travelled in much smaller groups, some of 24, others of 60; in those instances they travelled on regular trains. But similarly careful plans were laid to ensure that they arrived safely at their destinations.

Wives remaining behind were permitted to travel to the Albury railway station to bid farewell to their husbands. Wives had not always migrated to Australia at the same time as their husbands. One migrant, for example did not inform the I.R.O. officials or the Australian selection team that he was married as he was under the impression that only single men were being selected for migration. Certainly during the earlier stages of the scheme:

> Owing to the shortage of family accommodation selection ... was confined to single men and women and childless married couples or heads of families prepared to travel ahead of their dependants who would join them later.[42]

His wife did not come out till 1951 when he paid her fare to Australia.[43]

Wives who had migrated with their husbands either remained behind in holding centres in the south after their husbands had left for canecutting, or travelled with them up to North Queensland, and were accommodated at the holding centre for dependants in Cairns, while their husbands went to live at the cane barracks. Eventually the wives remaining in the south were either transferred to the Cairns holding centre or permitted to live with their husbands, the husband having notified the C.E.S. that he had suitable accommodation.[44] It could be weeks or even months before either transpired. Occasionally the cook in the displaced persons gangs travelling north on

41 AA: CRS BT60/1, 1946-1948; Q48/5437.

42 AA: CRS A445, 1951-1955; 179/1/6 pt 1.

43 Yugoslav canecutter I.D., interviewed 5 November 1984.

44 Ukrainian canecutter and canefarmer F.N., interviewed 3 November 1984.

the special trains was not a male but the wife or even daughter of one of the gang members.[45]

Seasonally between 1949 and 1951 trains offloaded an exotic cargo at quaint little railway stations dotted along the sugar belt. Waiting were anxious farmers. After the usual preliminaries, invariably numbed by food and drink, the migrant gangs were loaded on to the backs of trucks and made their way out of town. Behind twitching curtains curious eyes noted their passage. Jolted and tossed along the narrow corrugated roads between tall stands of pinkly flowering cane, they finally reached their homes for the next six months: the barracks, isolated and primitive.

45 See also Memorandum for Officers of the Commonwealth Employment Service, 1 February 1949. AA: CRS MP243/3 1943-1950, 1-14 p.6.

THE GOYA

One of the ships which transported displaced persons to Australia

BONEGILLA : the Commonwealth Employment Service

facing p.24

CANECUTTERS BARRACKS

On stumps, entirely clad in corrugated iron, with push-out windows: kitchen, and detached ablutions, are to the left.

facing p.25

CHAPTER 4

Habitation, Habiliment, 'Hard Tack' and Health

A few miles back Tiny had told him to watch out for the barracks. 'Just down off the track a bit, son. Got a shouse and a shower and an umbrella tree.' He had seen the building, set back from the railway. He counted eight doors under the long tin verandah roof and the usual kitchen at one end with a smokestack. 'We'll be six months in her - it'll seem like a generation'.[1]

1 R. Donaldson (*et al*.) *Cane!* London 1967, p.43.

On the first morning of the 1949 sugar harvest as thick mists banked up over the paddocks and nocturnal creatures scurried to their day-time resting places Branko was shaken awake from a fitful sleep. Deep, restful, obliterating slumber remained tantalizingly out of reach on those first nights in the barracks. The rompings and husky coughs and hisses of possums and the melancholy wailing of curlews punctuated his tossing and turnings on the narrow stretcher.

Though tired and anxious Branko set off on his first day of canecutting eager to be working and earning money. The ruddy glow of dawn light had just begun to suffuse the horizon. By nightfall of that day he would have been roughly initiated into the labour of canecutting and unbeknown to him it would have already begun to work the charm that would draw him back to the ripely beckoning fields each June for 20 seasons.

Over those seasons Branko would never stray far from the tropics. After his first years in Ingham he cut his way as far north as Mossman and finally on to Cairns to the last 'cut-out' day in a field that has since been swallowed by suburban sprawl. The aspects of barracks life and the canecutting job which will be described and which he experienced were those common to the far-Northern Region in the post World War II period up to the mechanization of the harvesting process.

It was to the barracks, quaint little structures overhanging riverbanks, tucked away under the shadows of mountains, that canecutters made their way on arrival in the sugar towns. John Naish's description of a canecutter's return to the barracks at the beginning of the season captured both the primitiveness and the changelessness of those structures:

> The barracks were the inevitable tongue-and-groove unceiled iron-roofed shambles of Old Queensland. He staggered up the four wooden steps to its saving grace, the long verandah, creaking with age and dryness. Already the feeling of timelessness, the sad ingredient in the twittering of birds, was making him uneasy. Was it that you always returned older? Was it that you always returned to further dilapidation never repairs? Did Ruf, who lived here through the slack, feel it too, feel the sudden restless surge of the past?... Mark trudged through the room that would be his, and dumped the great carton on the yielding trestle table in the galley. Ruf's fortnight's absence was like a ghost in the long room. That hanging safe that should have been swinging was still as an old, dead, leafless tree. A great web moored it eerily to the table, where a dusty clock insisted time had stopped at eleven o'clock long, long ago. It was the suddenness: from teeming town to hidden valley: from one extreme of life, which was people and beer and betting slips ... to the other ... in a barracks under the mountain ... bats flying silent through the brain ... silence injected into the veins like a serum making you giddy ... dimming the hornet buzz at the window ... or was it a tractor crawling on the flats.[2]

2 Naish, *The Cruel Field*, p.22. Similarly it was the isolation of the barracks which struck migrant cutters most forcibly.

Barracks were constructed of various materials over time: wood, brick, fibrolite and, most commonly, galvanized iron. They were usually raised above ground level on "stumps", like so many other domestic buildings in Queensland. Floors were of wood or concrete. There were several rooms, usually four or five for sleeping; at one end a room served as kitchen, identified from outside by the flue of its wood stove. Each room was to hold two men, the upper limit set by the *Workers' Accommodation Act*. A verandah ran the full length of the building. In barracks "low-set" a shower recess and laundry tubs might be located on the verandah. In barracks "high-set" on stumps these amenities might be in a structure separate but adjacent. Also adjacent as a rule was a rain-water tank and at a greater distance a small outhouse containing the pit-type earth closet. Windows were seldom glazed; ventilation was usually obtained by propping open hinged sheets of galvanised iron, freely admitting air, light and wildlife.

Each bedroom was equipped with bunks of some sort and the kitchen with cooking utensils. Perishable food was most commonly stored in an air-cooled safe suspended from a rafter. Lighting was usually provided by kerosene lanterns, infrequently by electricity.

The *Workers Accommodation Acts of 1915 to 1946* provided for the supply of this accommodation by the farmer free of charge and obliged him to furnish the barracks as described in that document and maintain it in a state of repair.[3] Officers of the Department of Labour and Industry would periodically check that standards were being maintained. However, one farmer asserted that prior to 1954 little or no supervision of barracks accommodation was carried out, but in that year "farmers were directed to keep barracks decent. The A.W.U. Rep. communicated this to the Cane Growers' Secretary who communicated it to the farmer".[4] Thereafter the roof had to the ceiled, fridges provided and a 'first aid kit' furnished. He described the barracks in the "early days" as "primitive".[5] Barracks were usually occupied by single men, but sometimes a married couple would share with one or more single men, the wife cooking for them all.[6] More commonly married couples would live in separate barracks, or rent accommodation in town. The barracks inhabited by a woman reflected her presence in cut-out wax paper decorating shelves, wardrobes constructed by stringing material on wire across wall corners, and gingham curtains at the windows.

Not all the canecutters living in one farmer's barracks need be cutting his cane. Some might be under contract to another farmer who would pay to have them housed.[7]

3 For the Act and amended regulations, see the *Producers' Review*, XL No.6, April 1950, p.45.

4 Yugoslav canefarmer M.G., interviewed 1 April 1984.

5 *Ibid.*

6 Problems associated with a canecutter's wife acting as cook are highlighted in the report of a social worker, Hazel Dobson, from Ingham: "Balt Problems", 12 August 1984 in AA: CRS A434, 1939-1950: 50/3/13 Lt 2.

7 Yugoslav canefarmer A.A., interviewed 6 March 1983.

Sometimes a canefarmer would befriend a group of canecutters and let them live in his barracks in the slack, even though they had been cutting and living elsewhere during the season.[8]

New migrants were usually shocked at the first sight of the barracks, finding them little better than a pigsty,[9] considerably worse than the way horses were stabled 'back home.'[10] When they entered the barracks they immediately noticed that "all normal conveniences were missing. Only bed in the room not very clean, no windows, just shutters, cold shower, primitive toilet. Kitchen very rough with old utensils".[11] Invariably there was no electricity or fridge and only one tap, or no running water at all. Nevertheless for a few the barracks were better than some of the places they'd lived in.[12] As time passed they usually tried to make barracks life a little more comfortable. One innovative gang "invented a contraption made up of a kerosene tin, rags and a pipe to heat water for a shower. They used sump oil because it burns steadily".[13]

Just as the barracks the canecutters lived in were basic and utilitarian, so too were their working clothes. Occasionally though, somebody would be adorned frivolously like Mark an engaging character of *The Cruel Field* who "strode up the furrow in nothing but shorts and a bowler hat he had come by lately. He wore it dented on one side..."[14] Essentially, the clothes a canecutter wore to cut cane were dictated entirely by personal preference. However, over time a virtual uniform evolved.

In a pamphlet issued to the migrant cutters they were advised to wear a brimmed hat, trousers rather than shorts, flannel and/or singlet and leather working boots or sandshoes.[15] The grey short-sleeved flannel shirt was common apparel of both farmer and cutter while the Jacky Howe or athletic singlet became inseparable from the popular image of the canecutter.[16]

In the dew of early morning, while loading the wet cane on to trucks, a long-sleeved shirt was usually worn. By the heat of midday most cutters had stripped down to singlet or even bare chest. Though trousers were advised most canecutters wore shorts. As the Jacky Howe was identified with the canecutter so too were the canvas sandshoes which were worn till the canvas rotted. These were rarely accompanied by socks. A multiformity of hats were worn: wide-brimmed felt hats as advised; canvas hats; berets; skull-caps; knotted handkerchiefs; and even swathes of material. Long-sleeved shirts

8 Yugoslav canefarmer M.G., interviewed 1 April 1984.

9 Yugoslav canecutter T.A., interviewed 14 May 1983.

10 Yugoslav canecutter D.N., interviewed 28 May 1983.

11 Yugoslav canecutter K.B., questionnaire completed early 1982.

12 Yugoslav canecutter and canefarmer A.P., interviewed 5 March 1983.

13 Yugoslav canecutter D.N., interviewed 28 May 1983.

14 Naish, *The Cruel Field*, p.71.

15 "Health Advice to Cane Cutters in the Sugar Industry", AA: CRS BT60/1, 1946-1948; Q48/5437.

16 See, for example, the cartoons "Northern Tourists" and "Retired" in L. Such, *Cane: a Book of Drawings by a Canecutter*, Gordonvale 1932; and Donaldson (*et al.*), *Cane!*, p.44. "He saw the purple-black cane and an army of men in grey singlets and slouch hats..."

and trousers, though hot, guarded against hairy-mary and cuts from trash.[17] The Jacky Howe or flannel, on the other hand were light-weight and absorbed perspiration. Similarly canvas sandshoes were light-weight, springy and wore well. Scanty head-gear was preferred. Canvas hats and material fabrications were favoured because they could be wetted and placed dripping on the head to cool head and face. The more scanty brimless type of cap was favoured for loading because the brim of a hat got in the way when loading and unloading bundles of cane from the shoulder. Other items that were worn were designed to guard against pain: fingerless gloves worn when cutting and padding for the shoulders when loading.

Canecutting required numerous sets of work clothes as clothing had to withstand the rigours of hard wear and frequent washing. Numerous sets of work clothes the displaced persons did not have. Branko, while relatively well clothed had managed to salvage precious little of his former life. An indistinct photograph of his uncle and aunt stiffly erect and unsmiling on their wedding day, and one of him as an infant mewling and clutching at air with tiny flailing hands were all the tangible reminders he had of home and family. While in Graz he had accumulated a few items of clothing; while docked in Port Said he acquired from an intrepid hawker an outfit of lightweight clothing that he was grateful to have for canecutting when the time came. However most displaced persons arrived in Australia with little more than the clothes they stood up in. A port with a pillow in it was in one instance the sum of a new arrival's wordly possessions.[18] Provision had thus to be made to supply the displaced person canecutter with not only everyday clothing but work clothes. The articles issued to them have been itemized elsewhere.[19] The subject of suitable clothing for the prospective displaced person canecutters produced much correspondence during the period 1947-1951 between the Department of Immigration and the Australian Sugar Producers' Association. It was the concern of that Association that displaced person canecutters be issued with clothing appropriate to canecutting, the Government issue being hardly suitable for such labour. Consequently, C.G. Fallon, Brisbane Branch Secretary of the A.W.U. (Queensland Branch Executive) upon request from the Queensland Cane Growers' Council communicated to the Minister for Immigration that the following clothing was required for sugar workers: "two pairs of ordinary working trousers, four athletic singlets or working flannels, four pairs of light working boots or sandshoes" and "one working hat".[20] The outcome was that new canecutters were issued with one pair of sandshoes and two pairs of working trousers; the rest of the list was disregarded. The Queensland Cane Growers' Council reimbursed the Department of Immigration for the items supplied and the Council itself later redeemed the outlay by deducting the corresponding amount from the cutters' wages. Despite those plans not a few

17 This apparel was more common in the days of cutting green cane when Jean Devanny wrote, "Most cutters wear long pants and a flannel or singlet in the green cane, the pants to protect them from the sharp leaves and hairy mary - the prickles that cover the cane". *By Tropic Sea and Jungle*, Sydney 1944, p.91.

18 Yugoslav canecutter M.L., interviewed 15 May 1983.

19 Above, Chapter 3.

20 C.G. Fallon, Sec. A.W.U. Queensland Branch, to Calwell, 13 Jan 1944. AA: CRS A445, 1947-1951; 179/1/3 Pt 3.

migrants found themselves ill-clothed for canecutting and had to venture into the paddock in what clothing they could muster. Overdressed or underdressed as many of those new cutters went to work, they must have been a source of amusement ot Australian observers. One group of Polish ex-soldiers was supplied with surplus army dress during their stay at Bathurst Army Camp. Though they had been selected for canecutting it had not been suggested to them that they would require shorts or light footwear. Consequently some of these went into the field on the first day dressed in "Canadian tank unit battle dress made out of heavy wool, long boots of dark brown colour - laced, long gloves - light cream colour, woollen shirt" and "battle dress top".[21] At the other extreme some Lithuanians used to cut and even *load* cane clad only in underpants![22]

While it was necessary for canecutters to wear suitable clothing it was of greater importance to eat great quantities of well-cooked, nutritious food. Hazel Dobson, a social worker who wrote a report on the problems experienced by 'Balt' gangs employing female cooks, concluded her report with the statement that "Canecutting is one of the hardest jobs in Australia, and men cannot cut and load cane unless they are properly fed".[23]

Food might be bought by the gang or the cook from the nearest store, or ordered from and delivered by stores' representatives calling at the farm; either system might be conducted on a cash or a credit basis. Alternatively the farmer might buy food on a list supplied by the gang and the cook and recover his costs on producing dockets at the end of the week.[24] The cost of major food items such as bread and meat were sometimes deducted from the canecutters' wage by the Cane Growers' Executive and the paid directly to the butcher and baker.[25] In the period 1947-1951 gangs with as many as eight members were common in the far north. When a gang had no more than six members they either took turns to cook the three main meals of the day or employed a cook who spent a quarter of each day in the field.[26] Larger gangs employed a full-time cook.[27]

Even full-time cooks were often unqualified, especially in migrant gangs working their first season. The cook received an equal share of the cutting money. In addition, each canecutter issued to the cook money to be spent on food, or authorized him to order the necessary food on their behalf. If they felt he was cooking unsatisfactory meals, or wasting the money issued to him they had reason to be dissatisfied.

21 Polish canecutter A.S., interviewed 8 November 1984.

22 Lithuanian canecutter G.Z., interviewed 30 October 1984. However the discomforts of loading did eventually drive one to wear shoulder pads his wife made for him. "They were not to know it, but to locals this skimpy attire was regarded as slightly indecent, although whether it was a manifestation of European backwardness, or daring modernity, was unclear." Burrows & Morton, *Canecutters*, p.114.

23 AA: CRS A434, 1939-1950; 50/3/13 Pt 2, p.3.

24 Yugoslav canecutter D.N., interviewed 28 May 1983.

25 Yugoslav canefarmer M.G., interviewed 1 April 1984.

26 He was not, however, legally obliged to do so. See "Working Conditions" in AA: CRS A445, 1951-1954; 179/1/4 Pt 4.

27 Sugar Industry State Award: Food, etc.; *Q. Industrial Gazette*, 30 June 1948, p.690.

Each day the cook had to prepare three hot meals and to carry tea and sandwiches to the field for morning and afternoon smoko. In addition, wood for the stove had to be cut, water carried for various purposes and the common areas of the barracks kept clean and tidy. On the week-end, the cook and cutters often had a respite from each other, with the cutters eating in town.

The food eaten by canecutters had to be nutritionally rich and energy giving. Oranges, bananas, pawpaws, pineapples, mangoes and other fruits growing on the farm were eaten plentifully. Breakfast was as substantial as the other meals with eggs,bacon and steak commonly on the menu. Steak appears to have been a favoured food for all meals and was eaten in great quantities: "I came home from the paddock last night at half past six and sat down to my supper. I ate about a pound of fried steak".[28]

In the poem "The Canecutter's Lament" a greater portion of what was lamentable was the food and the cook's disposition!

The first six weeks, so help me Mike
We lived on cheese and half boiled rice,
Doughy bread and cats-meat stew,
And corn beef that the flies had blew.

The Chinese cook with his cross-eyed look
Filled our guts with his corn-beef hashes,
Damned our souls with his halfbaked rolls
That'd poison snakes with their greasy ashes.

The cane was bad, the cutters was mad,
The cook had a hob-nailed liver,....[29]

As the poem indicates,the temperament of the cook and the quality of the food was as much a determinant of a good season as the condition of the cane or the gangs' relationship with the farmer. However,the pamphlet giving health advice to new migrant canecutters expressed the main necessity for eating well most succinctly: "It is very important to eat well. You cannot work well unless you eat well".[30]

On arrival in the sugar towns the new migrant gangs were sometimes taken to an eating house for a meal. For many it was their first non-institutional meal for many a year and the memories of the aroma and taste of that meal remain indelibly.[31] If the farmer had helped them to procure food stores on the journey to the farm, they could prepare their first meal on a farm in North Queensland for themselves. Occasionally a hospitable farmer would invite the gang to eat their first evening meal in his home.[32] Thereafter the gang had to make its own arrangements, which could cause problems

28 Devanny, *By Tropic Sea and Jungle*, p.89.

29 "The Canecutter's Lament", in W. Scott (comp.) *Complete Book of Australian Folklore*, Sydney 1976, p.124: a somewhat bowdlerised version.

30 AA: CRS BT60/1, 1946-1948; Q48/5437, p.1.

31 Ukrainian canecutter and canefarmer F.N., interviewed 3 November 1984.

32 Yugoslav canecutter V.V., questionnaire completed early 1983.

for any gang. For migrants there was a twofold difficulty: the risk of getting an inexperienced cook, and adjustment to an unfamiliar diet. If a migrant recalled that the food was "good" in the first season it was usually because the cook was a fellow national.[33] In the first weeks of cutting a 'green' gang's wages might not "... even pay for 'tucker' ...."[34] On the initial journey to the barrack one Polish gang stopped to buy food at a convenient store. They were so bedazzled by the array and quantity of food displayed in the store that, after having lived for years on the brink of starvation, they found themselves buying everything in bulk until "the three tonner was full of it".[35] Of course they *just* managed to cover the food bill with their first pay! If a gang had a professional cook who fed them superbly even that fortune was not appreciated when the food bills had to be paid from new-chum pay packets: "Food was good" commented one Yuguslav canecutter, "as we were fortunate to have a cook by trade who served us with great meals a good variety and various courses at every meal. It cost us plenty as matter of fact first few pays we got very little left after paying for food".[36] While the elected cook in Branko's gang was no chef he was able to muster by intuition and memory a meal reasonably faithful to his mother's cooking. Nevertheless as all migrant cooks were to discover, traditional foods sat uneasily during sweltering afternoons of canecutting.[37] Anglicizing his cooking made meals less palatable but more digestible.

> The food that the immigrants are accustomed to may not be suitable if they were employed in the strenuous work of cutting cane. In any case, they will no doubt require their food cooked in a certain way and these immigrants no doubt have certain habits understood only by their fellow workmen. We find that one of the main reasons inexperienced cane cutters would not remain in the cane fields was the "tough" conditions and mainly it was not a question just of the quantity of food, but one also of quality.[38]

Occasionally gangs were accompanied by female cooks; two instances were reported by interviewees. In the sugar industry generally the practice had long proved unsatisfactory, and in fact the Award did not permit it. But

> ... both employers' and employees' organizations (i.e. Cane Growers' Council and Australian Workers' Union) have for some time by tacit agreement "winked at" the employment of female cooks and have signified their agreement to the proposal to include married couples in cane gangs. The women would not actually be placed by the Commonwealth Employment Service, as cooks, but could cook by local arrangement and share in the profits of the gang ...[39]

33 Yugoslav canecutter M.L., interviewed 15 May 1983.
34 Yugoslav canefarmer M.G., interviewed 1 April 1984.
35 Polish canecutter A.S., interviewed 8 November 1984.
36 Yugoslav canecutter K.B., questionnaire completed early 1982.
37 Yugoslav canecutter and canefarmer M.M., interviewed 21 October 1984.
38 R. Muir, Gen. Sec. Q.C.G.C. to Calwell, 3 Nov 1947. AA: CRS A445, 1947-1951; 179/1/3 pt 3, p.1
39 "Allocation of Workers to Sugar Industry and Rocket Range", Memo C.C. Watson, Dept. of Immigration, 14 April 1948. *Ibid.*

At first the Department of Immigration desired to side-step the provisions of the Award for several reasons. Firstly, it was thought most unlikely that male cooks would be available amongst the displaced persons. Secondly, it was agreed that:

> gangs for cane cutting comprise eight men and a cook, i.e. an allocation of 550 male Displaced Persons will yield 61 gangs including cooks. If married couples are allowed to work, the husband on cane cutting and the wife as a cook, then 61 gangs can be made up from 427 single men and 61 married couples, thus making available for other employment 122 single men who would other wise be employed 61 as cane cutters and 61 as cooks.[40]

However by the 1949 season, it became policy that only male displaced persons were to be selected as cooks for canecutting gangs.

One of the major reasons why women proved to be unsuitable as cooks was the nature of the job and the conditions under which the cook had to work. The social worker Hazel Dobson who wrote a report on the problems experienced by 'Balt' gangs employing female cooks described the work as being:

> ... very hard and hot for a woman involving very long hours, isolation, constant work, cooking for 8 or 9 men who need practically five meals a day, including two hot meals, and the carrying of tea and sandwiches twice to the fields - sometimes a long distance from the barracks and over wet ground. Wood must be cut for the fuel stove and water must be carried.[41]

The situation was aggravated by the fact that in many of the cases observed by Dobson, the women were young girls with "no experience in cooking or ordering for a large group of men."[42] An added point of contention was the sharing of earnings.[43]

A male cook shared equally in the canecutters' earnings but he cooked, kept house and frequently worked in the field. For a woman cook the men felt obliged to cut wood and carry water as it was heavy work for a woman, especially if she was pregnant as were several of the women of Hazel Dobson's study. The cutters resented sharing equal earnings with somebody part of whose work they had to do and who often was a bad cook into the bargain.[44]

40 *Ibid.*

41 "Balt Problems", report 12 Aug 1948. AA: CRS A434, 1939-1950; 5/3/13 pt 2, p.1.

42 *Ibid.*

43 One immigrant's experience was a case in point. He came up to Ingham as part of a gang of eight. With them travelled their cook, the daughter of one of the members. In his opinion it wasn't 'good business' to have a man cook let alone a woman cook. Yugoslav canecutter and canefarmer M.M., interviewed 21 October 1984.

44 Neither of the two women cooks cited in the sample cooked for a canecutting gang after the first season.

The 'Health Advice' pamphlet issued by The Queensland Cane Growers' Council not only advised the migrant canecutter to eat well but listed in great detail a variety of afflictions which could torment the cutter during the season. The pamphlet concluded, not altogether convincingly: "don't get the idea ... that canecutting is unhealthy work. It is not. Canecutters are an extremely healthy group of workers, working in the sunshine and open air ...."[45] How to give realistic advice without frightening off potential recruits was a problem the Council had struck in canvassing the idea of a leaflet to be issued by the Commonwealth authorities: "hasten to avoid giving the impression that workers in cane districts are subjected to any more physical discomforts than are associated with other industries. They are not".[46] Although this was too rosy a view, some of the ailments suffered by a canecutter were temporary. But it was difficult to credit this in the opening days of the season. With the felling of the initial stool of cane on the first Monday of the new season the pain and blisters started:

> Like crops of small button mushrooms, the first blister-buds appeared on the hands, grew tight and burst. Sword-edged cane leaves cut into the skin drawing blood in fine beaded lines and a host of muscles began first to throb, then to stiffen and finally settle to a raw burning torture. As if at a given signal, the flies of Queensland left their dunghills and moved in on the cutters' eyes, ears and noses, and stuck inquisitively to the corners of their mouths and the air, trapped by tall cane, became thick, hot and full of sultry weight.[47]

Muscle cramps and pain though worst during the hardening-up period were experienced by canecutters throughout the season. They could suffer "... terrible aching limbs all the time".[48] It is understandable that muscles would protest, for the canecutter spent most of his day bent with one arm in constant motion: grabbing, cutting and throwing down three stalks, each weighing perhaps three or four pounds and up to 10 feet in length.[49] In addition he had to manually load an average of six to ten tons of cane in a day. To do this he had to lift and carry to the trucks bundles of 12 to 15 stalks of cane; some bundles weighed up to 100 lbs. Furthermore, portable rail tracks[50] had to be carried to where the cane had been cut, in itself a strenuous activity for: "Each length is sixteen feet and requires a maximum effort of strength from two men. When you've carried a dozen of these maybe a hundred yards each at the end of the day, you don't feel very good towards the business.[51] There was no relief possible

45 AA: CRS BT60/1, 1946-1948; Q48 S43F, p.2. As an example of official fatuousness, cf. the parting advice of the recruiter of migrant cutters, D. Callighan: "If you start clapping your hands now, by the time you reach Ingham your hands will be tough enough to cut cane". Yugoslav canecutter and canefarmer M.M., interviewed 21 October 1984.

46 Q.C.G.C. circular to District Executive Officers. AA: CRS A445, 1947-1951; 179/1/3 pt 3, p.6.

47 Donaldson (*et al.*), *Cane!* p.72. Set in Innisfail just before the Second World War, this book gives detailed and unmatched descriptions of canecutting despite a style rather highly-coloured.

48 Yugoslav canecutter V.V., questionnaire completed early 1983.

49 Donaldson (*et al.*), *op. cit.*, p.72.

50 See below, Chapter 8.

51 W.B. Tyrell, "The Canecutters are at Work", *North Australian Monthly*, September 1954, p.27.

for the initial painful muscular fatigue; the hardening-up period had to be worked through. In the story *Cane!* "Tiny and Frank were stretched out on the concrete still clothed, filthy with sweat and dust, and unsmiling".[52] Cutters remember seeking relief for both muscular pain and the sting of raw blistered hands by hanging their hands down on the cold floor of the barracks.[53]

Blisters were a particularly painful temporary ailment suffered by old and new cutters alike in the first few weeks of the season. There was little relief to be offered though 'new chums' were usually told to "... go out and piss on 'em sport".[54] or treat them with methylated spirits. However, experienced canecutters, like Emery of *The Cruel Field*, knew that time and continued work were the only effective cures:

> Canecutters are wrong: urine doesn't cure blisters. It may ease them, but apart from retirement there is only one cure: the friction of continued labour. The blisters go deeper and deeper, unobtrusively become callouses, and then one day the cutter finds himself trimming the great corns with a razor blade to stop them splitting any further.[55]

In time hands came to resemble "leather - soles of boots".[56]

On occasion the knife would hit a vine or stone and bounce back gashing the skin. The effectiveness of the cutting action was in the wrist. Initially, the 'new chum' experienced jarring until the wrist became supple. In the early morning the cutter often worked soaked to the skin by rain, or from loading wet cane,[57] suffering chills, colds and influenza. The sharp edges of the sugar cane leaves scratched and cut the skin; hairy-mary became imbedded in the skin and caused rashes. Not uncommonly cuts and irritations would develop into 'sugar boils'. Working in wet canvas shoes caused tinea; sweat-sodden clothes coupled with summer humidity encouraged prickly heat. Insects too were a bane on the canecutter's life: march flies, bees and mosquitoes. Not infrequently in the days of cutting green cane canecutters died of Weil's Disease.

> ... the virus was spread by rats urinating in the wet ground and on the cane stalks, and invaded the cutters through abrasions received while handling the cane trash ... if the cane [was] burned before harvesting the trash would be removed and both the cane and ground would acquire a degree of sterility.[58]

As a result, districts where cane was burnt prior to cutting, the incidence of Weil's Disease was diminished markedly. However, the odd case did still occur.[59]

52 Donaldson (*et al.*), *op. cit.*, p.73.
53 Yugoslav canecutter J.P., interviewed 31 March 1984.
54 Donaldson (*et al.*), *op. cit.*, p.75.
55 Naish, *The Cruel Field*, p.69.
56 Yugoslav canecutter D.N., interviewed 28 May 1983.
57 Tyrell, *op. cit.*, p.27.
58 D. Menghetti, *The Red North*, Townsville 1981, p.30.
59 Yugoslav canecutter M.L., interviewed 15 May 1983. Two interviewees contracted Weil's Disease: one, advised to refrain from canecutting for two years, never returned to the field except for one month as a 'dummy'; the other contracted the disease in 1956 and was still cutting in 1962.

By the afternoon, the paddock became a "stifling wet oven".[60] In the shadeless paddock the unburnt cane acted as a windbreak while the sun beat down relentlessly on the backs of the men. For the fair-skinned sunburn was an added aggravation to the hardening-up process. Emery, a character in *The Cruel Field*, a man of fair complexion had:

> ... burnt, peeled, burnt again; but had once more got used to the heat by the end of November. He was tanned and weary; his eyes were too sore and bloodshot to read or write; but he was thankful to have no serious ailments as the end of the season approached.[61]

Initially the migrants had the extra burden of acclimatization and, in many cases, accustoming their bodies to labouring. The displaced person canecutters were from every walk of life. Some had no experience of rural life or manual work. One had been a teacher, the son of affluent city dwellers; in his gang were an opera singer, a chef and an architectural student.[62] Fortunately, most commenced cutting their first seasons in the North Queensland winter. Perhaps more migrant gangs would not have lasted the first season if they had started work mid-season in the heat of a tropical summer.[63] As it was, they were wearing singlets to work, sweating profusely and diving into a nearby river to cool off when the farmers were still rugged up in jumpers.[64] Discomfort was commensurate with effort expended. So also was money earned; every member had to work hard and consistently for a gang to earn good money. One migrant, unique among those interviewed in experiencing no physical pain in four months canecutting, admitted that he had not worked hard: his gang broke up because of poor earnings.[65]

Canecutting could result in permanent ailments. In the days of manual loading it was said that a former canecutter could always be recognised by his sloping shoulder, caused by carrying and loading heavy bundles of cane. Some suffered permanent back problems in later life, possibly because they made a habit of lifting bundles heavier than was wise. Now and then a canecutter lost a finger, or sustained a wound requiring stitches and leaving a permanent scar. Working shirtless, as many did, in the tropical sun day after day could bring sun cancers in later life. Ex canecutters often blame arthritic and rheumatic pains on their canecutting days.[66]

In later life Branko had to have "sunspots" removed from his face. Arthritic pain dogging him as the years passed he attributed to working constantly in sweat-soaked clothes, often in cane dripping with dew, sometimes in drizzling rain. But he views his

60 Donaldson (*et al.*), *op. cit.*, p.74.

61 Naish, *op. cit.*, p.171.

62 Polish canecutter A.S., interviewed 8 November 1984.

63 Yugoslav canecutter and canefarmer M.M., interviewed 21 October 1984.

64 Lithuanian canecutter G.Z., interviewed 30 October 1984.

65 Czech canecutter R.C., interviewed 8 March 1985.

66 Yugoslav canecutters T.Z., interviewed 3 January 1983; J.P., interviewed 31 March 1984; V.V., questionnaire completed early 1983.

ailments philosophically, for old age brings all manner of physical deterioration: if not sunspots and arthritis, then something else.

Many canecutters experienced excellent health during the season. One observed that "he was fittest and healthiest when he was cutting".[67] Some, in peak physical condition, thrived on strenuous physical labour. Emery, the principal character in *The Cruel Field*, recognised that his buoyant sense of well-being was due not only to "the change in the weather, the coming of a kind of hot Australian spring; it was also a matter of fitness. He had never allowed himself to become badly out of condition; but there was a difference between merely fit and being superlatively fit. Now he felt supreme fitness."[68]

Canecutters gave up for reasons other than ailments or ill-health incurred at the end of the knife. Marriage, a more secure job, advancing age, mechanization were more common reasons.[69] Migrant cutters who, like Branko, continued to cut for up to two decades, are still vigorous and healthy men.

There were canecutters who ate irregularly and badly; there were those who consumed alcohol in prodigious quantities and for whom every Monday was the beginning of the season all over again. For a good many canecutters youth and endurance were the qualities that enabled them to cut cane, not sound health. If canecutters appeared healthy it was in part because only the healthy or the young and strong could endure the toil.

67 Yugoslav canecutter K.B., questionnaire completed early 1982.

68 Naish, *op. cit.*, p.69.

69 Yugoslav canecutter T.A., interviewed 14 May 1983.

TABLE 4-1: MAJOR AILMENTS OR ILLNESSES

CANECUTTER	AILMENT OR ILLNESS
A.P.	Back problems
A.S.	None
B.I.	Back and knee problems (he blames equally his P.O.W. experiences)
D.N.	None
F.N.	Weil's Disease
G.M.	Back problems
G.Z.	Hurt back lifting rails
I.D.	Sore wrists
J.P.	Arthritis; vericose veins
K.B.	Back problems
K.M.	Arthritis
M.L.	Ulcer; Weil's Disease
M.M.	None
R.C.	None
T.A.	None
V.V.	Arthritis: back problems

TABLE 4.2:

CANECUTTER	NUMBER OF SEASONS CUT	AGE IN LAST SEASON	YEAR OF LAST CUT	REASON FOR LEAVING CANECUTTING
A.P.	8	25	1957	Left canecutting to manage a farm.
A.S.	23	54	1971	Age. Secured a job a the Sugar Terminal.
B.I.	18	52	1967	Thought 18 years canecutting were enough. Coming of mechanization.
D.N.	3	28	1952	Married. Felt canecutting was not a suitable way of life once married.
F.N.	9 weeks + 1 month	40	1949 1957	Contracted Weil's Disease in first season. In 1957 had purchased a mechanical loader but cut as a 'dummy' for one month for the gang to whom he was contracted to load.
G.M.	11	32	1961	The work was too hard.
G.Z.	5	30	1952	Married. His wife inherited part ownership of her parent's farm; he worked on that farm till retirement.
I.D.	3	43	1951	Sore wrists were bothering him.
J.P.	11	54	1969	School offered him a job as a yardman.
K.B.	4	25	1952	Offered job at Brewery as a clerk. Could see opportunity there for advancement.
K.M.	17	46	1966	Coming of the harvester. By 1966 all the good farms used mechanical harvesters. Age.
M.L.	11	37	1962	Ulcer burst; offered a job at the Brewery.
M.N.	2	26	1949	Canecutting had no future; employed for only half the year. Wanted job permanence once married.
R.C.	4 months	21	1951	The nature of the work; inability to earn money in the job; back problems.
T.A.	6	40	1960	Sick child; moved to the Tablelands for his health.
V.V.	17	39	1967	Coming of the mechanical harvesters.

OUTSIDE THE BARRACKS : Freshwater near Cairns, 1949

This gang included an engineer, a truck driver, a barber and a saxophone player: clothing and headgear are equally varied.

A LITHUANIAN GANG

The female cook is the wife of a member

CANECUTTER MONUMENT, INNISFAIL

Tram rails and 'canestalks' form the balustrade, with cane knives and files attached; jets of water issue from 'waterbags' on the pedestal.

facing p.41

CHAPTER 5

The Image of the Canecutter

To gather in the harvest
Of seven million tons -
Queensland calls the hardiest
And stoutest of her sons.....
The cutters toil like heroes
Where creeks and rivers meet -
Knocking down the stately Eros
And the Trojan long and sweet.
They make no bones about it
Bright silver is their aim -
Their sanity - I doubt it -
Who will say they love the game...[1]

1 "The Cane Harvest", in D. Sheahan, *Songs from the Canefields*, Canberra 1972, pp.116-7.

Canecutting, gang labour seasonal in character, generally conjured up images of mateship and adventure. Going canecutting had some of the romance of joining the Foreign Legion or pioneering on the frontiers: attributes attractive to a young man eager to experience 'life'. Unlike Branko many young men were soon overwhelmed by the prodigious physical effort demanded by canecutting. Those who persevered at the labour were regarded as either beast of burden or superhuman hero for having done so, images which were colourfully immortalized by literature.

Certainly those who lived in the small sugar towns in the era of manual canecutting will attest to those days having a colour and romance of their own. Canecutters did find mateship and adventure in canecutting. However, the physique of the real canecutters, their day to day routine, were to some degree misrepresented by literature. Often writers unnecessarily embellished the physical pain experienced by new cutters; spectacularly emphasised leisure times spent carousing, womanizing and gambling; and unduly stressed the animosity between the cutter, the cocky and the cane inspector. Neither hero nor beast, the canecutter was an ordinary man earning a hard living. But canecutter literature does have the great merit of recording in detail a way of life and labour which has ceased to exist, one which no man living will be able to describe from personal experience before many more years have passed.

No man was born for canecutting: "one of the toughest, roughest and hardest jobs in Australia".[2] A farmer who saw many canecutters come and go remarked that a man's size did not determine whether he would make a good cutter or not.[3] John Naish of *The Cruel Field* claimed that large men didn't last long in the job because they had enough trouble carrying their own weight let alone shouldering cane.[4] There were exceptions of course such as the book's character Snowy Hutchinson, a veritable colossus. Esme Gollschewsky also observed that "paradoxically, some of the gun cutters were hugely *fat men....*"[5] She graphically described what she saw as the essential canecutter:

> In fact, he was never the bulging-muscled, athletic, Noble Savage type beloved of the cartoonists and others. The best and most enduring cutters tended to be men of average height, slightly built, ... their muscles stringy and sinewy like the tendons of a scrub turkey, the skin of the arms, legs, face, and neck burnt by sun and wind and rain and roaring fires to the colour of old mahogany, their tongues impious, their manners to women

2 Tyrell, "The Canecutters are at work", p.27.

3 Yugoslav canefarmer M.G., interviewed 1 April 1984.

4 Naish, *The Cruel Field*, p.21.

5 E. Gollschewsky, "The Yesterdays and Today of the Sugarcane Industry", *The Bulletin*, 12 April 1969, p.75.

> gallant, their honesty rather too apparent and serving to conceal a quick-wittedness and admiration for all forms of skullduggery.[6]

Esme Gollschewsky's mention of the 'Noble Savage type' is a reference to what seems a not uncommon view of canecutters as being apart from the rest of humanity. Jeff, a character of *The Cruel Field* made a bitter statement to this effect; "'Human?' said Jeff, laughing. 'You ask the Nagonda socialites whether we're human. Canecutters are bloody animals, Danny.'"[7] Jokes of this nature were not rare:

> A tourist bus was passing through Cairns cane-fields. A dear old lady saw some canecutters in action. 'Goodness me,' she said, 'Whatever is that?' 'They're canecutters, madam,' the bus driver answered. The dear old lady shook her head. 'Dear me,' she said 'and they look just like men, too!'[8]

Neither were cartoons uncommon. Les Such, ex-canecutter and one-time cartoonist for the Sydney *Bulletin* penned a priceless one.[9] In a *Cairns Post* article written in the last days of the canecutter (1973) an official of the Cairns District Canegrowers' Executive praised the canecutters of his association. But in so doing he raised the question of their humanity: "The cane cutters were part of the human race to me. They could be bloody difficult. There were some rogues, some good, honest triers."[10]

The same article made reference to the "... bronzed muscular cane-cutter".[11] Because of the nature of the job: hard, back-breaking, outdoors labour, popular conception had the canecutter sun bronzed and 'muscle bound'. As the job was one of physical skill and endurance, mental acumen was perceived to be superfluous. And it was thought that men of intelligence would not be drawn to such an occupation. A farmer's wife once heard "it to be said that if a canecutter has plenty of brawn and muscle he doesn't need much more".[12] And canecutters themselves sometimes agreed that "all you need are muscles,no brain".[13] Nevertheless the way of life appealed to men of varying intelligence and amongst the canecutter ranks were writers, former doctors, university students and office workers.

6 *Ibid.*

7 Naish, *op. cit.*, p.61.

8 C. Morton, "Sugarcane Waste, Fertilizer Bags and Human Canecutters", *North Australian Monthly*, December 1957, p.43. Clive Morton wrote a column, "Sugar in N.Q.", for the *North Australian Monthly*. His book broke new ground in devoting a chapter to displaced person canecutters. Chapter 10, "Balts, DPs and Reffos".

9 Such, *Cane*, unpaginated.

10 L. Bolton, "Memories before the 18th Doll", *The Cairns Post*, 12 October 1973. My emphasis.

11 *Ibid.*

12 M. Graham, "Our Canecutters", *North Australian Monthly*, February 1960, p.36.

13 Yugoslav canecutter I.U., interviewed 29 May 1983.

NORTHERN TOURISTS
A.D. 2032

Canecutters born in the tropics were not the only ones to evince brawn and tan for "Innisfail and other cane growing centres were alive with fit, sunburned young men from Italy, Spain, Yugoslavia and other countries and Australians from down south".[14] When cane was bad, and even more in the panic as the season neared its end, the cutter would often demand, and sometimes get, any price he fancied. Then the terms applied to the canecutter were less complimentary: "'industrial pirates', 'quick-money boys', 'industrial blackmailers', a bad and savage breed whose notoriety was everywhere acknowledged."[15]

Ray Lawler's play "The Summer of the 17th Doll" was the first in its genre to immortalize the Australian canecutter. The character depicted was "boisterous, hard-working, hard-playing", one who could gamble or spend his pay in a weekend. This popular canecutter archetype was often disputed by canecutters themselves. An ex-cutter and one time mayor of Bundaberg saw in Lawler's cutters the men of a bygone era who had disappeared by the 1930s. He claimed that the canecutters of the post-War era were steadier, and often local-bred or based.[16]

In contrast to the popular image of the canecutter as a man of brute strength and subhuman demeanour is the reaction of journalist Larry Foley to the Innisfail canecutter monument. Foley found the monument beautiful and moving:

> The knotted muscles of the canecutter spell strength, the well-defined ribs exertion, and there are grace, dignity and resolution in the bowed head, and down case eyes and the firm jaws... But he could step down from his pedestal and take his place with the team in the nearest field today; in 80 odd years he has not changed. ...it looked so right in marble; it made him eternally clean and cool and so made up for what the living flesh of those he symbolised had always endured.[17]

There were many who saw as subhuman the blackened, sweaty men in the fields, cursing at the twisted cane and urinating on painfully blistered hands. Others who appreciated the demands of the labour, the physical fitness required, the gang camaraderie, and the eager seasonal return, may have idolized the canecutter as a "slashing awe-striking hero".[18] Somewhere in between was the reality: ordinary men working expertly at a hard job. The rewards were ordinary enough too: mateship and susbtantial remuneration.

As for Branko and the immigrant canecutters upon whose experiences this account is based: Branko on his arrival in Australia was fair-skinned, with hair the lustre of gold. Short and thin, he exuded boundless energy. His boyish appearance and blue-eyed candour engendered sharp argument among his countrymen in Bonegilla over his suitability for membership of their gang. Canecutting under the harsh tropical sun

14 Bolton, *op. cit.*, p.2.

15 Naish, *op. cit.*, p.205.

16 E. Johnston, "Canecutters' award whittled down to a one-man stand", *The Australian*, 21 December 1977, p.3. See also Bottomley, "Sugarfield Scenes", p.30. "Old tradition of high life and heavy drinking during big-wage cutting season is dying, and wild types of early days are being replaced by sober, saving, ambitious workers who make good use of earnings."

17 L. Foley, "Five, Six, Pick Up Sticks", *Bulletin*, 7 December 1963, pp.23-24.

18 Naish, *op.cit.*, p.14.

eventually wrought changes: a sinewy strength and a burnt butter complexion. The displaced person canecutters on whose experience this book is based range from five to six feet in height; most have skin browned by the sun but few are sinewy and gnarled. All are well-spoken, with tongues infrequently impious. Many were mischievous and irresponsible but then in those days they were young and full of youthful exuberance. Do they look like ex-canecutters? In some cases only their hands indicate a life of physical toil. Several are elegant, stand proudly tall and can be pictured walking out of a coffee house of old Europe. Some are shy, reticent, mildly truculent, but all are articulate, aware, interesting. Indeed the post World War II migrant canecutters were as varied as the faces of humanity.

CHAPTER 6

The Ganger

Dave. His cobber. Never done this before. Won't again, not in Tiny's gang. Dave had known trouble in his time, strictly weekend though, by Sunday night he was back in the barracks .... So long as he pulled his weight, Dave's problems were his own business. When not, such as right now, they was ganger's business.[1]

1 Donaldson *(et al.)*, *Cane!* p.136.

Cane could be cut by the farmer himself, by a single hired hand, or by groups ranging from two to eight men. Displaced persons were mostly formed into gangs of the larger sizes - five to eight - prevailing in the Northern Region. (South of Ayr, gangs of two to four men were normal.)[2]

Gangs were usually formed in one of two ways. In the first, one man selected others to work with him, aiming at a gang of hard workers. Alternatively men could form a gang spontaneously, "on the 'birds of a feather' principle",[3] selecting one of their number to be the ganger. If found wanting, he might be dismissed by the gang, or replaced by another member. Once formed a gang might remain together, and even cut for the same farmer, season after season.

Once the gang was formed the ganger's responsibilities were extensive. Some were administrative: filling-in time sheets, discussing tasks with the farmer and generally acting as spokesman. When the cane was 'bad' it was he who negotiated with the farmer for a special rate. Other responsibilities were for man management: in particular letting a man know if he was not pulling his weight, more generally maintaining harmony in the field and in the barracks.[4] His earnings were the same as those of all members of the gang.

> The job of ganger was to negotiate prices with farmers and inspectors, to liaise with unions, to ensure that enough cane is being burnt, ... to negotiate accommodation and update facilities, to see that the cook is efficient and not waste time or goods and to make sure that he is able to set an example in the field.[5]

A passage from John Naish's *The Cruel Field* highlighted the personal qualities required of a ganger:

> Mark didn't like the onus of finding a cut switched on to him so adroitly. He wasn't cut out for leadership, decisions, responsibility. It suited him to leave the ganger's job to Ruf as usual: he was a calm sort of bastard who never did his block in an argument. Besides, you never got a zack extra for all the planning and worry.[6]

2 R. Muir and E. Pearce to A.A. Calwell, 9 January 1948. AA: CRS A445 1947-1951, 179/1/3 Pt 3.

3 R. Schlomowitz, "Team Work and Incentives: the Origin and Development of the Butty Gang System", *J. of Comparative Economics*,3,(1979),p.48.

4 Yugoslav canecutters V.V., questionnaire completed early January 1983; J.P., interviewed 31 March 1984; D.N., interviewed 28 May 1983; T.Z. interviewed 3 January 1983; T.A., interviewed 14 May 1983.

5 Yugoslav canecutter K.B., questionnaire completed early 1982.

6 Naish, *Cruel Field*, p.16.

It was the ganger who approached the farmer to request a cut. While the farmer might ask around the district whether he was a good worker (and refuse if the response was unsatisfactory)[7] he had no say in the membership of the gang. That was entirely the ganger's prerogative. The farmer might know nothing of the other members of the gang he had engaged until they reported for work.[8] Farmers allocated displaced persons in their first season had even less say.

Migrants who went straight to canecutting from the Reception and Training Centres usually did so in gangs of their own countrymen: in succeeding years they often worked in mixed gangs.[9] In the post-war period European gangs predominated in the north while Australian gangs were more usual from the Burdekin south. A migrant canecutter who cut 18 seasons in the north did not work with Australians until his last years of cutting.[10]

Canecutters were paid by the ton cut, at a rate set for the district at the beginning of the season.[11] Conditions underfoot or in the cane that impeded cutting entitled the cutters to seek an extra rate. As seen above, it was for the ganger to approach the farmer. Failing agreement, resort would be had to the Cane Inspector, with results sometimes humorous - at any rate in the retelling. A Lithuanian told of asking the Cane Inspector for 6d. a ton on a particularly bad field. The Inspector replied that "the sun would rise from the west before he'd give them 6d." A price of 9d. was eventually designated after the A.W.U. Organizer was called in.[12] One Polish ex-cutter while waiting for the Cane Inspector to be called asked the ganger of a neighbouring Australian gang what price he should ask. The Australian anticipating a laugh at the Pole's expense suggested an exorbitant price. Coincidentally the Polish ganger, an ex-serviceman, had earlier been invited to join the R.S.L. where he had struck up an acquaintance with the Cane Inspector in question. Thus when the Inspector did call to designate a price he and the ganger chatted amicably and finally as he was leaving the Inspector asked the ganger what price he wanted. Told the advised price he replied that that was what he would have suggested himself. At lunch time the Australian gang wandered cockily over to the Pole's barracks only to be informed that the Cane Inspector had granted the advised price. The Australians returned to their barracks deservedly deflated.[13]

The ganger in Branko's gang was a man quick of intellect and temper. Formerly a musician, his pugilistic face and his penchant for displaying his considerable physical strength veiled his exquisite mastery of the violin. Music summoned by his bow assumed a life of its own: it shimmered, danced, tumbled and soared. His pug-like

7 Sugar Industry: State Awards, Canecutters Agreements. *Queensland Industrial Gazette*, 30 June 1948, p.693. A cutter with a bad record might be blacklisted throughout an area. Australian canefarmer S.B., discussion October 1984. An "unsatisfactory industrial record" might also result in refusal of a cut. *Producers'Review*, 15 April 1950, p.45.

8 Yugoslav canefarmer M.G., interviewed 1 April 1984.

9 Yugoslav canecutter J.P., interviewed 31 March 1984; also Polish canecutter K.M., interviewed 9 November 1984.

10 Yugoslav canecutter V.V., informal discussion 8 October 1984.

11 See below, Chapter 10.

12 Lithuanian canecutter G.Z., interviewed 30 October 1984.

13 Polish canecutter A.S., interviewed 8 November 1984.

face was transformed with quicksilver changes of emotion as he and his violin merged. His mates chose him to be ganger because of his intellect and strength without thought of his fiery temper and love of showing-off. They were not good attributes where a cool head and appreciation of the ethos of teamwork were critical.

Teamwork - equality of effort and output - was paramount in cane cutting. The argot had evolved two words of pejorative connotation: 'dummy' and more particularly 'weed' to describe those whose effort and output were unsatisfactory.

CHAPTER 7

The New Chum

A ridiculous pride swelled within him. For a week he'd been cutting in the gang proper and not in a row apart, and he could more or less hold his own. He fell in behind the others with a flush of excitement rising round his ears.[1]

1 Donaldson *(et al.)*, *Cane!* p.120.

The cane Prices Board determined how many tons of cane a farmer could harvest and how many men he would need. In times of unemployment such as in 1953 and again in the 1960s a quota system was applied. The calculated number of tons a man could cut was reduced and gangs expanded in proportion. A three man gang might cut the number of tons previously designated for a two man gang.[2]

Cane-cutting operated on a collective-piece-rate payment system:[3] all members of a gang shared equally in the joint earnings.If a weaker gang member cut six tons to the gun's ten, he received the same sum in his wage packet at the end of the fortnight. Naish highlighted these issues in this conversation from *The Cruel Field:*

> 'Then it's the same old gang.' Ruf frowned. 'Hard to say,' he said. 'It's supposed to be a six-man cut according to the estimates. We may have to sign on a dummy or two.'
>
> 'What!' cried Mark. 'You don't believe all that Mace bull in the paper about surplus men and quotas?'
>
> 'No,' replied Ruf calmly. 'I believe they'll be just a few men short. It's just that they might not like us signing on two men light. I been thinking we ought to get someone else.' 'To hell with them!' cried Mark. 'We can handle it ourselves. This is our chance to make a quid!'
>
> 'We'll make a quid soon enough,' said Ruf patiently. 'But look at it this way: if only four of us go to the Sign-on, and Peter turns up with two men, there'd be nothing much we could do and you know what that'd be, don't you?'[4]

Obviously four able to cut a six-man assignment would have a lucrative contract. Against the risk that gangs might take on more than they could manage, the Award provided for the farmer to add members to a gang unable to meet its commitments.[5] At sign-on a gang could be directed to increase its size, or a Cane Inspector could order it on a visit to the farm. The gang might then be forced to accept members not of its own choosing,[6] as Mark, a character in *The Cruel Field* pointed out:

> 'Reckon Meester Forrester serious 'bout another man Mark?' asked Tony. 'What you think I'm trying to recruit someone we know for?' replied Mark. 'We'll probably wind up putting on a new-chum. Some bloody New Australian who's never seen cane before.'[7]

Ordered at sign-on to enlist another member, a gang could try to find one of proven ability. But if confident of its own prowess it might seek a "dummy" - a man without experience - simply to make up the number. If party to the ruse the dummy would drop out by arrangement after a few weeks: an unwitting dummy, finding the going too tough, would leave after a similar span. In either case the gang counted on being

2 Yugoslav canefarmer A.A., interviewed 6 March 1983.

3 See Schlomowitz, *op. cit.*, for the development of the Butty Gang System in Queensland and canecutting as a collective-piece-rate payment system.

4 Naish, *op. cit.*, p.16.

5 *Queensland Industrial Gazette*, 30 June 1948.

6 Mills tended to encourage additions to the gang in the interests of continuity of supply, and the A.W.U. in order to maximise its own revenue.

7 Naish, *op. cit.*, p.48.

able to demonstrate within that time that it could fulfill the contract with the original number - and with greater earnings. A dummy would also be recruited to hold a place for a member late getting back from a slack season job.

Any member of the gang who could not keep to the pace expected of him within the gang was labelled a 'weed'. In this extract Naish defined a weed and hinted at the friction a weed within a gang could cause:

> 'There was a young feller in the ward here; kid named Danny Hoover. They reckon he's a good toiler.' He coughed awkwardly. 'Um - hasn't cut cane before but -'
>
> 'You nuts or something?' broke in Mark. 'You suggesting we take in a kid who's never cut before? What the hell you-'
>
> 'Take it easy,' said Ruf, 'take it easy! He'd just be a dummy. If he's got it in him, okay. If he hasn't he'll quit within a fortnight: weeded out. See what I mean?'
>
> 'I don't like carrying weak reeds,' said Mark unconvinced, 'even for a fortnight.'[8]

Most men were conscious that the nature of the job and the system of payment demanded teamwork. The greater a man's output the higher the reward for the gang and for each member. Conversely the earnings of the gang and of each member were diminished by substandard output by any of them. Contempt for weeds and the drive to maintain, if possible improve upon, a gang's expected output put great pressure upon new chums. Those who could not match the required pace usually dropped out of their own volition, impelled by self-recrimination, on top of the initial physical agonies.[9] Devanny described what happened to:

> ... inexperienced men going into a strange gang. They're afraid they won't be able to keep their end up. A man is expected to pull out if he can't keep up with the gang. If he doesn't pull out on his own and he's really bad, he's told to get out.[10]

Jean Devanny was a New Zealand born writer and political activist who wrote numerous fictional works, a number of which were set in Queensland. Amongst those were *By Tropic Sea and Jungle* (1944), and *Sugar Heaven* (1936). In the former, Chapter xi entitled "The Cane-Cutter's First Day" gives a rare detailed description of the work of canecutting.

Both books are unique for their portrayal of the life style and people of North Queensland at a time when other authors failed to see any romance, beauty or value in that subject. I draw on both books even though they describe canecutting as it was practised in the 1930s and 1940s.

The gang usually worked together, lived together, socialized together, for seven months. This demanded some degree of harmony if not close friendship among

8 Naish, *op. cit.*, p.16.

9 Schlomowitz, *op. cit.*, p.48.

10 Devanny, *By Tropic Sea and Jungle*, p.90.

members. This harmony, for the most part, evolved when there was a rough equality of ability in the field.[11] Weeds and shirkers created disharmony and even gang-splits. Danny in *The Cruel Field* was acutely aware of that. He was cutting so ineffectually that he:

> ... trailed by chains. Tony watched him from the lea of the tractor shed: hitting more frantically than the others, suffering more, sweating more: but cutting less cane and - this was what deepened his scalding frenzied shame - earning exactly the same share of pay. This was what caused the splits, what had caused the thousands of gang-splits down through the years: the pay was as equal as two envelopes; but even a rough equality of ability was arrived at only by ordeal, strain and stress, trial and distress; by the dropping of the weak in the mud and mist of the harsh young season.[12]

John Naish wrote from firsthand experience; few canecutters would have failed to identify with his graphic account.

> The slowest man always worked harder than the others and worried his heart out into the bargain. He himself had known what it meant to come home too sick and tired to eat, too sore and tired to wash properly. He had known the restless nights and the nightmares, the muscle-cramp, the blisters, and the constant self-reproach. He had known the agony of trying to load bigger bundles, bigger bundles, faster and faster and faster ... and still getting left behind ... and burning after tea when he felt half-dead from want of rest ... and waking with a start to the horror of the dawn and another day ...[13]

Canecutters usually felt that they had mastered the basic skills of the job after three weeks but for a few it could take from six weeks to a few months to feel that same mastery. Certainly after the first season they should have felt no doubt about carrying their weight in the gang. The first day has been variously described as 'pain' or 'misery' or even 'hell' and it was not unusual for novice canecutters to want to give up after their first day. Not all canecutters would ever become 'gun' cutters, but once hands and body hardened up the cane could be attacked with verve. One interviewee spoke of looking forward to each new season with excitement, as to a picnic.[14] Similar sentiments were expressed in *The Cruel Field* when Jeff tried to encourage Danny, the new cutter, who was ready to give up. He described his own experiences, the other gang members' attitudes, and finally how:

11 For a similar observation see Association of Agriculture, *A Sugar Cane Farm in N.Q.: Farm Study Scheme*, London 1963, p.15.

12 Naish, *op. cit.*, p.33.

13 Naish, *op. cit.*, p.62; Tyrrell, "The Canecutters are at Work", p.27; Donaldson *(et al.)*, *Cane!*, pp.72-3.

14 Yugoslav canecutter M.L., interviewed 15 May 1983.

> ... they smiled, and gave me a cup of rum, and a pep-talk just like I'm giving you. And you know what that was?' ... 'The turning-point! I was in a better frame of mind, and able to rest. I was hardened up, not suffering so much. And there was the encouragement of knowing I was improving. And, believe it or not, when Christmas come I was sorry to see the season end, and there was Ruf and Mark, asking me to cut with them again next year .... And that's how it's gonna be with you, Danny; you wait and see![15]

Despite looking forward to each new season, a canecutter could only cut as long as health and stamina permitted.[16] Jean Devanny named thirty four as the ceiling age for a canecutter,[17] but it was not uncommon for a cutter to be still working at forty, despite the physical demands and monotony.

Branko was forty-five years old when he finally decided to retire from canecutting. Twenty years earlier in those first agonizing days of cutting when he plodded back to the barracks in the shadow of evening dazed with weariness, grazed and bruised by his attempts to master the field of short, straggly and grass-choked cane, he would not have credited that he would see out the first week let alone the first season. For anyone to choose to cut for twenty seasons would have seemed foolhardy beyond belief. Nevertheless once the cane improved, his body acclimatized to the rigorous labour, and he had received a few pay packets that left a bit to spare, his jaundice quickly evaporated. Next season, no longer a raw new chum he returned eagerly to the North, beckoned by the charms of the tropics: the sweet lure of the sugarfield life.

15 Naish, *op. cit.*, p.62.

16 See Chapter 4 above.

17 J. Devanny, *Sugar Heaven*, Sydney 1936, pp.27, 37. Australian canefarmer S.B., informal discussion February, 1985, disagreed with Jean Devanny's assertion. He stated that 34 would, in many instances, be the *peak* age period for *top* cutters. Many were in their prime in their late 30s or early 40s due to their experience.

CHAPTER 8

Canecutting: the Occupation

I'll say for the curious, that cane cutting would be a good occupation for a man with the hide of a rhinoceros, the strength of a bull, and the agility of a monkey.[1]

1 Such, *Cane*, Preface.

The new season was heralded by the sign-on when the farmer and his prospective gang would meet to seal their contract, usually about the second week of June.

The sign-on[2] might be conducted at the picture theatre, at the town hall, a mill, or the Canegrowers' office. Along with gangs already formed, attending the sign-on with the farmer as arranged by their ganger, there would be individuals hoping to be recruited into an incomplete gang. "There were always more canecutters than jobs offered. Some left the district immediately to look elsewhere for a cut", but many remained, knowing that there would be those who "just couldn't take the job ..."[3] and looking to replace them. Only those holding union tickets would be employed and canecutters were expected to have purchased the ticket before signing a contract.

Present at the sign-on were the A.W.U. Representative, Cane Inspector, Cane Growers' Secretary, Ambulance Officer, bankers and storekeepers. John Naish captured the tempo, the apprehensions, the atmosphere of the sign-on day:

> That was the first time the sign-on had been held in the Pacific Cinema. It seemed a lot of bother to go to in order to get a few hundred scrawled signatures on a pile of gentlemen's agreements. But at least it gave the flag-sellers, storekeepers, ambulancemen, and bankers a chance to get their hands on a bit of it, and the Nagonda News duly announced 'A Successful Sign-on' .... Now and then a small farmer, with only one or two cutters, was able to get the business over with, but things were proceeding disjointedly: the larger gangs were hard to marshal, and a growing crowd stood outside the doors waiting in the sun for expected members to turn up, from the stores, from the two pubs. It was only ten-thirty: nobody was in a desperate hurry: there would be rushing and tearing enough when Monday came. A farmer who drove off to find a missing cutter would invariably return to find someone else had 'just gone up the street a minute'. For the most part the farmers greeted one another and stayed in a group, all smiles discussing their record crop, lauding the great varieties. And the cutters, strangely silent, nodding and grinning occasionally, lounged around the entrance, pretending nonchalance, tired from the previous season which had gone well into January. The new-chums were apprehensive: they had been promised pain.[4]

In addition to the normal contract between canecutters and farmer, displaced persons were bound by the two-year condition imposed by the Commonwealth Government. Although warned that disciplinary action could be taken against those who reneged, some left canecutting after the first season, or even during it, with impunity. One, a passenger on the *Mohammedi*, contracted Weil's Disease in his first season and left canecutting on medical advice, but worked as a general field labourer.[5]

2 Sugar Industry State Award, *Queensland Industrial Gazette*, 30 June, p.695.

3 Yugoslav canefarmer M.G., interviewed 1 April 1984.

4 Naish, *The Cruel Field*, p.23.

5 Ukranian canecutter and canefarmer F.N., interviewed 3 November 1984. Only two others interviewed left for other work within the first year.

There were, however, occasions when the C.E.S. enforced the agreement. A compatriot of Branko who also arrived on the *Mohammedi* in May 1949 was with a gang in his second season when, dissatisfied with the farmer they were contracted to, they split up. A few remained with the farmer; several moved to a contract in the same district; Branko's compatriot and his friends travelled a short distance down the coast to a cut they heard was available. The farmer housed them and then took them to town to sign-on. There the C.E.S. officer was waiting: he compelled them to return to their original district, but not to the same farmer, under threat of extending their two-year contract. They had been under the impression that they were honouring their commitment so long as they remained canecutting, and knew of friends who had given up canecutting inside the two years and gone to work in Brisbane without being followed up by the C.E.S.

The general feeling among displaced persons was that the two-year contract should be fulfilled. But some were not happy about rural work which took no amount of educational and trade qualifications. A Pole who cut cane for a remarkable 23 years conveyed the frustration of an intellectual whose present status is grossly inconsistent with his former pre-war life and work. He criticized the Australian authorities for using the immigrants for their brawn, instead of taking advantage of their skills. He argued that if they had done so the migrants would have been better able to improve their lot and would have made a more substantial contribution to the Australian way of life. He said that "he could have achieved more if he had started teaching or entered the army. He would have been more benefit to the country than working as a slave cutting cane."[6]

Nevertheless he cut cane for over two decades by choice rather than from force of circumstance. He illustrates the ambivalence of canecutters towards their work. Memories of good times are spiced by humour and pathos and capture all the bittersweet intangible reasons why men went back season after season. A Lithuanian remembered his gang coming home drunk one night and going out in that state to load the next morning's rake: a clownish parody starkly silhouetted by streaming moonlight.[7] A Pole recalled the beauty of the mountains, the cool crisp mornings as they began to load the day's rake; the sense of mateship as they talked during the walk to work and then started the day's tasks. At those times it was "nice" to be in the paddock and no more so than when the Italians would break into gusty song as they worked.[8]

Branko, like many migrant cutters, went into the field for the first time totally ignorant of what to do or what to expect. Others had been given prior warning that "'You won't die; but you'll almost die'".[9] And certainly recalling the memories of the

6 Polish canecutter A.S., interviewed 8 November 1984.

7 Lithuanian canecutter G.Z., interviewed 30 October 1984.

8 Polish canecutter K.M., interviewed 9 November 1984.

9 Lithuanian canecutter G.Z., interviewed 30 October 1984.

first time the blisters bubbled in dozens, the shoulders ached in protest and an all-consuming pain enveloped the body one cutter felt that "... it nearly killed him".[10]

While still in the Reception and Training Camps several had been warned by other new immigrants not to go cutting. Various reasons were offered, the most common being that there were too many snakes and that canecutting was a dirty job.[11] And indeed the most frequent adjective used by ex-canecutters to describe the job was 'dirty'. One commented that "they didn't say that he would get as dirty as he did."[12] Canecutting comprised three major tasks: burning, cutting and loading. Burning cane was dangerous; loading required strength, speed and skill; cutting "knack and rhythm".[13] Burning was done on Sunday, Tuesday and Thursday evenings. The amount burnt would provide enough for two or three days cutting. Burning cane before cutting had several advantages. Historically, the reason why cane was burnt was in order to lessen the incidence of Weil's disease.[14] Furthermore "it cleaned the trash and weeds, got rid of snakes which were plentiful, made the cutting much easier and complied with sugar mills demands to have clean cane for crushing".[15] Burning became universal practice during the war because the speedier harvesting that resulted compensated slightly for the paucity of labour.

Burning cane was spectacular and dangerous; Branko went to each burn of his 20 years of canecutting with a fearful heart. Burning was usually carried out in the evening when the wind had died down and the dew on the cane reduced the risk of the fire getting out of control. Burning could also be a lengthy process. The average paddock was not all burnt at once. A fire break was made by forcing two adjacent rows in opposite directions to separate what was to be burnt from what was to remain unburnt. Under normal conditions "a couple of men could walk briskly down between two drills of cane, leaning them back, doing the job in twenty minutes...."[16] Cane is pliable and can be made to lean at quite an angle. Taking a length of cane, each man would hold it horizontally and push down on the rows to be separated. Another man would follow the break pushers raking the trash away in order to make a clean break.

All that was needed for a burn were matches, water-soaked sacks and armfuls of trash. The burn was started at the break: the corner was lit and then one or two men would make a torch of trash and take the fire down the break. Another might take the fire down the opposite headland, especially if a standing paddock, young cane, or a riverbank needed protecting. Since he was firing against the wind - backburning - he would be given a few minutes start. The two men would then keep pace and, having reached the end, run the fire round the face of the paddock, meeting in the middle. As the fire burned away from the break the other men would file into the break and

10 Yugoslav canecutter and canefarmer A.P., interviewed 5 March 1983. Yugoslav canecutter J.P., interviewed 31 March 1984 said that "... he nearly died!"

11 Yugoslav canecutter D.N., interviewed 28 May 1983.

12 *Ibid.*

13 Association of Agriculture, *A Sugar Cane Farm in N.Q.*, p.15.

14 See Chapter 4 above.

15 Yugoslav canecutter K.B., questionnaire completed early 1982.

16 Naish, *op. cit.*, p.29.

A 'BURN', Mossman, 1955

The man in the foreground is holding two water-soaked sacks

facing p.60

MOSSMAN 1955

Red Hill, outside Cairns, 1958

LOADING CANE

(Note the spacing at trucks along the tramline.)

around the perimeter of the burnt area beating with wet sacks at the still smouldering grass and trash. For a time the fire would continue at its normal speed:

> ... and then, as the air above the last triangle became heated and the draught swept in from all sides, the fire screamed upward in a great pyramid of flame, lighting the headland like day.... Scores of bandicoots, rats and mice scurried and hobbled from the inferno.... The fire gave a last exultant scream and collapsed, leaving the ring of burning grass. For a few moments there was the sound of beating sacks, the coughing of men, and then nothing but the faint clicking of burned sticks in the blackness.[17]

Throughout the fire 'floaters' (flying pieces of burning trash) had to be keenly watched, for if they landed in other paddocks they could set off further fires. Similarly, animals fleeing across the break, fur alight, had to be driven back into the fire rather than endangering the cane to be left unburnt. After the burn canecutters came "home at the end of the day, blackened like coalminers from the burnt-cane..."[18] Cutting burnt cane, men were exposed to the sun and sheltered from the breeze.

> Before the war, ... a block of cane was attacked from the south or from the east, so that the men got the benefit of the south-easterly breeze, and often worked in the shade of the standing cane. Nowadays, they have to start on the opposite side and work towards the wind. In this way, when the next burn occurs, the wind carries the sparks across the land already harvested. Inevitably, the unburnt cane acts as a windbreak and the men have the sun on their backs, with no shade.[19]

Burnt cane stalks remain undamaged; even the uppermost green stalks survive the blaze, only singed. However, burning marginally lowers the sugar content of cane. In burnt cane left standing for over 48 hours the sugar content starts falling in proportion to the time left standing. Therefore it was important that no more cane should be burnt than would be cut, loaded and received at the mill within two days at the outermost. Similarly cane burnt accidently had to be cut as soon as possible. Then the farmer was often forced to employ additional labour in order to avoid loss.[20] Branko's gang, as was usual, was shown how to burn cane the evening before it commenced work and was taught how to cut and load cane by the farmer on the first day of cutting.

Canecutters could start the day loading or cutting as they chose, but there had to be two loading shifts in each mill district as the mills could not supply enough trucks to allow all farms to load at the one time. Some cutters preferred to load in the cool of the morning, others in the afternoon when the cane was dry and would not slip as

17 Naish, *op. cit.*, p.31.
18 Foley, "Five, Six, Pick up Sticks", *p.23.*
19 Association of Agriculture, *op. cit.*, p.17.
20 *Queensland Industrial Gazette*, 30 June 1945, pp.692-4.

it was being carried, nor feet slide on a wet ladder. For farmers afternoon loading was marginally preferable as cut cane left overnight for loading the next morning suffered a slight loss in sugar content.

Loading was the most laborious part of the canecutter's job, and the first to be mechanised. Writing at the end of the 1959 season Leslie Roberts noted that efficient mechanical loaders were in operation in all districts[21] and maintained that canecutters had actively encouraged the innovation.

> As the machines began to appear cutters in many areas refused to continue to load cane manually ... insistence upon being relieved of the strenuous burden of hand loading.[22]

Loading required *speed* as Jeff pointed out to Danny in *The Cruel Field*. He advised him "... not to bust a gut lifting big bundles, because *speed - speed* was the only way midgets could load as fast as the long men."[23] Cane was not loaded in a haphazard manner on to the trucks but had to be piled in a 'scientific' way so that stalks did not work loose and "fall off as the truck sways and rattles in the long trains over the miles of bumpy tramlines to the mill".[24]

The cutter rolled a bundle of stalks of cane, containing perhaps 12 to 15 stalks onto his foot; he then raised one end of the bundle; encircled the bundle with his arms, and manoeuvred the bundle onto one arm then rolled it on to one shoulder. He carried his bundle, at a brisk speed to the truck onto which it was thrown. As the bundles of cane accumulated, the cutter had to load from a ladder which made the task even more arduous. The cutter carried his short ladder from truck to truck as he went.

Differing methods of placement of cane on the truck applied for short and long cane. When loading long cane it was *single-tiered*. That is, one row of stalks would reach the whole width of the truck. The next row would be loaded directly on top with the butts (thick ends) pointing the opposite way.

Diagram 1: Cane loaded 'single-tiered'

21 Three years later it was stated that "in the areas north of Townsville hand-loading of hand-cut cane remains the standard practice." A.S.P.A. *Annual Report*, 1962, p.14.

22 L. Roberts, "Another of the Vanishing Australians", *North Australian Monthly*, November 1959, pp.9-10. Mechanical loading not only lightened the work of the canecutter but it also enabled him to increase his output markedly; some were then cutting 20 tons a day. Despite the reduced rate for cane loaded by a mechanical loader, greatly increased earnings resulted.

23 Naish.*op. cit.*, p.63.

24 Foley, *op. cit.*, p.24.

When loading short cane the stalks were *double-tiered* (or overlapped). The butts pointed outwards while the tops overlapped in the centre of the truck.

Diagram 2: Cane loaded 'double-tiered'

Once loaded a chain was thrown over the cane and pulled very taut with a 'key'. Each truck would be carrying approximately 2-3/4 tons of cane.[25]

Dishonest or lazy cutters could load the trucks without observing the 'science' of loading; this was called 'crows nesting' a truck. To the untrained eye the truck would look adequately loaded, but in fact the bundles were punctuated by holes, which altered the weight of the truck of cane markedly.[26]

The task of loading could be made tortuous if the cane was crooked as John Naish describes:

> They climbed to the top rungs of the ladders next day, limping up with the wayward sticks of the great bundles catching in their clothes, in the rungs, in the load itself, the bent sticks mercilessly pinching their arms and necks. And they knew their straining and struggling was not being rewarded by heavy loads: from the side, they could see right through the enormous piles: they were towering loads of cane-and-air, and when the ratchets groaned the truck-chains cut deeper and deeper as if the loads would be cut in two. Indeed, many half-sticks dropped off before the trucks were moved, and many more would fall on the jolting journey to the mill.[27]

Once all the trucks were loaded the farmer hauled them over the portable tracks to the main line whence they were hauled by steam locomotive to the closest mill.[28]

The portable track was laid by the gang before loading: in the evening if loading was to be done next morning. It was the second most arduous task in canecutting. Tracks might belong to the farmer himself or be supplied by the mill. It was contingent upon the Cane Inspector to ensure that each farm was provided with its daily quota of trucks and was equipped with an adequate quantity of portable rails. The common

25 "Single-tiered" and "double-tiered" are terms used by Jean Devanny, who described loading and other cane cutting tasks in *By Tropic Sea and Jungle*, pp.91-93. See also Burrows & Morton, *The Canecutters*, pp.51-55. Although their description is of green cane cut and loaded in the Tully area in 1928, methods changed little in the subsequent twenty years.

26 Devanny, *op. cit.*, p.92.

27 Naish, *op. cit.*, p.198.

28 The method described was generally consistent over the region Mossman to Ingham. Different loading methods applied in other areas.

quota of trucks was three trucks per cutter per day. The farmer was responsible for laying the 'corner' (the tracks from the main line to the property), for bringing empty trucks to the paddock and for hauling them full to the main line. A docket (consignment note) was placed on the trucks bearing such information as the name of the farmer; names of the canecutters; variety of cane; and paddock designation. The trucks would be weighed at the mill and the cutters paid per ton of cut cane.

Once the morning's rake had been loaded canecutting would commence. The gang harvested blocks of cane in predetermined stages. If the gang was harvesting for a group of growers it would cut out blocks of cane for each grower in an agreed rotation. The block that was to be harvested was cut in 'trams' - each of approximately 18 drills. The ganger set the pace by tackling the first three drills[29] to be cut of the first tram. He commenced cutting and threw the cane down into the next drills: the cane of the second and third drills being thrown down onto the cut cane of this first drill. After he had cut half a dozen stools in each drill the next cutter commenced cutting in the next three drills. Within a few minutes the whole gang was at work, working in a staggered formation. When the ganger reached the end of his drills he walked back the length of the cut drills topping the cane lying on the ground. This task completed, he took up position at the next uncut drills which placed him immediately behind the last member of the gang and so the routine continued.[30] Alternatively, he might cut several yards along the drills and then walk back topping the cut cane, and continue this cutting and topping until he reached the ends of the drills. Then, rather than walking back down the drill, he would commence cutting, at this same end, the uncut drills immediately next to where the last member of the gang would emerge from cutting his first three drills. The order in which the men cut behind the ganger was determined by prowess

29 In the days of cutting cane green, in shorter varieties of cane, one drill only, or two drills simultaneously, were cut. In the 1950s, when longer varieties became more usual, cutters commonly cut three drills simultaneously.

30 In a gang of six, each cutting three drills, this would place him in the first drills of the second tram. See Diagram 3. How long it took to cut one tram depended on the length of the drills. If the drills were long it might take two days to cut one tram. Similarly, depending on the time it took to cut one tram, the gang might cut one tram and subsequently load it; or cut two trams and then load each consecutively.

CUTTING CANE

On the left a man is cutting left-handed; the caneknife held by the man in the centre is sharply bent for more efficient cutting.

Note the staggered formation of the three cutters.

TOPPING CANE

The stalks in the foreground have been topped: Gordonvale, about 1962.

CUTTING 'LYING-DOWN' CANE

Freshwater near Cairns, 1956

facing p.65

and speed. A 'new chum' may have improved so much in a season that other gang members would have to give precedence to him.[31]

On occasion migrant gangs were instructed in the old style of cutting: one stalk at a time, topped before dropping. Compounded by inexperience, this ensured meagre earnings. In the two instances related by interviewees old hands took the new chums under their wing, teaching them to cut several sticks simultaneously and top on the ground later.[32]

The portable rails were laid up the centre of the tram[33] and trucks hauled up and spaced along the track. Experience enabled the cutters to calculate how much cane lying on the ground would fill one truck.[34] The trucks would then be loaded from either side. Cut stalks were thrown to the ground so that the 'tops' pointed away from the rails. Therefore, the stalks of cane from the nine drills of cane lying on one side of the rails would be pointing in the opposite direction to the stalks of cane from the nine drills of cane lying on the other side.[35]

Each canecutter was equipped with a cane knife by the farmer, who was also obliged to provide water bags and files. The cane knife consisted of a wooden handle and long blade of highly tempered steel, not more than a thirty-second of an inch in thickness.[36] The blade was about 11 inches in length and five to six inches in width at the end, tapering to two and a half inches at the handle. Handles ranged from six to 15 inches in length depending on personal preference. During the period under discussion, the long handled knife was preferred to the short handled knife which was more popular when cane was cut green.[37] At the very end of the blade was a hook-like projection designed to strip leaves off the stalks of cane cut green.[38] Cutters frequently

31 In reality, the order was never as strictly regimented as described here. Normally, in a gang there was a rough equality of prowess - so the members would keep pace with one another. In the 'good' part of the season that would evolve into a game: for some, the 'chase' was one of the attractions of the work. Surprisingly, the ganger need *not* have been the fastest member of the gang. Yugoslav canecutter V.V., informal discussion 8 October 1984.

32 Yugoslav canecutter D.N., interviewed 28 May 1983; Lithuanian canecutter G.Z., interviewed 30 October 1984.

33 See Diagrams 4 and 5.

34 Two and a half to three rails per one truck usually measured enough cane to fill that truck. (Each rail measured 16ft. 6in.). When the cane was short it would take more rail length to fill the truck so the rails had to be uncoupled and shifted more frequently.

35 See Diagrams 4 and 5.

36 J.P. Frings, *The Australian Cane-Sugar Industry: From Virgin Soil to Consumer*, Brisbane n.d., p.13.

37 "The Magic Grass", *People*, 19 February 1958, p.36.

38 Association of Agriculture, *op. cit.*, p.17.

Diagram 3: Cutting order and alternative topping procedures

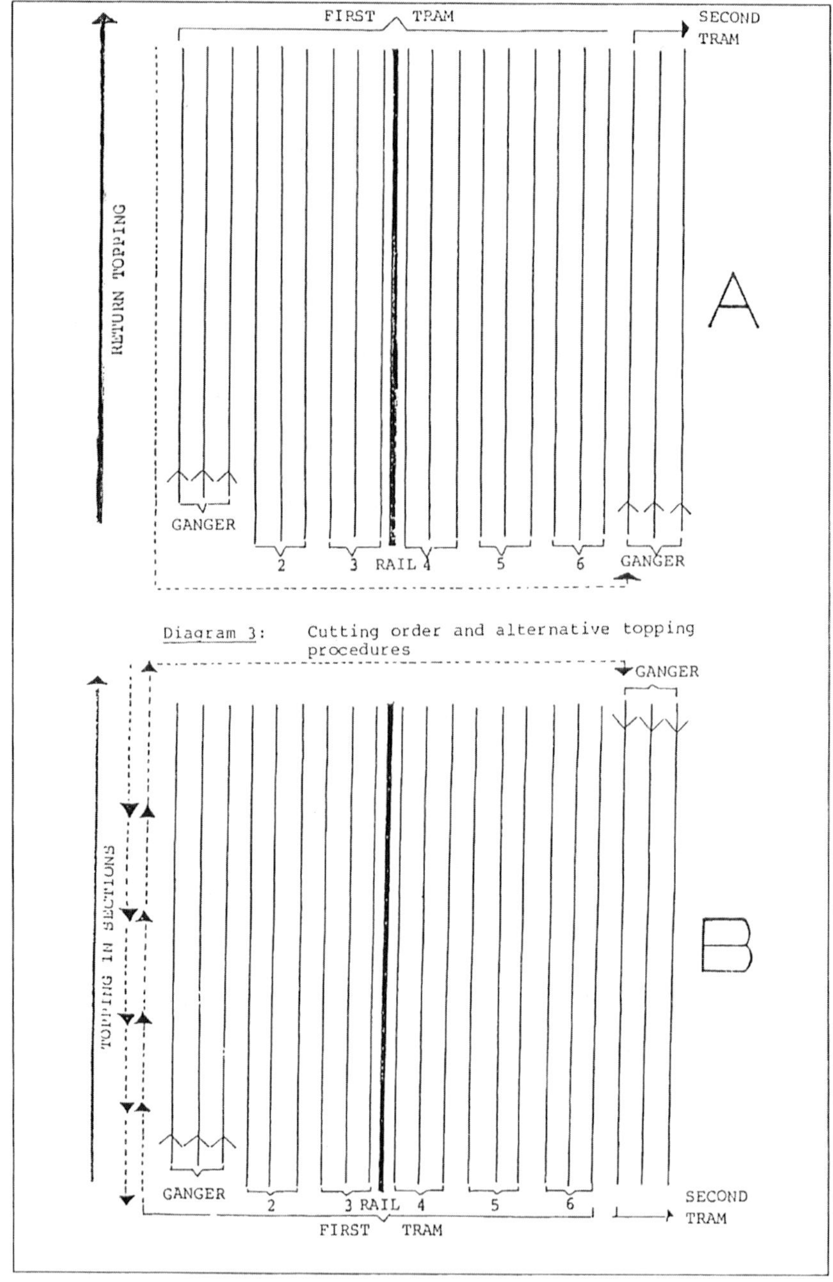

LAYING PORTABLE RAILS

Red Hill, outside Cairns: 1958

PORTABLE RAILS IN POSITION, Gordonvale 1964

Smoko is being taken on an empty truck

facing p.66

LOADING CANE MECHANICALLY

Ingham area, 1956

facing p.67

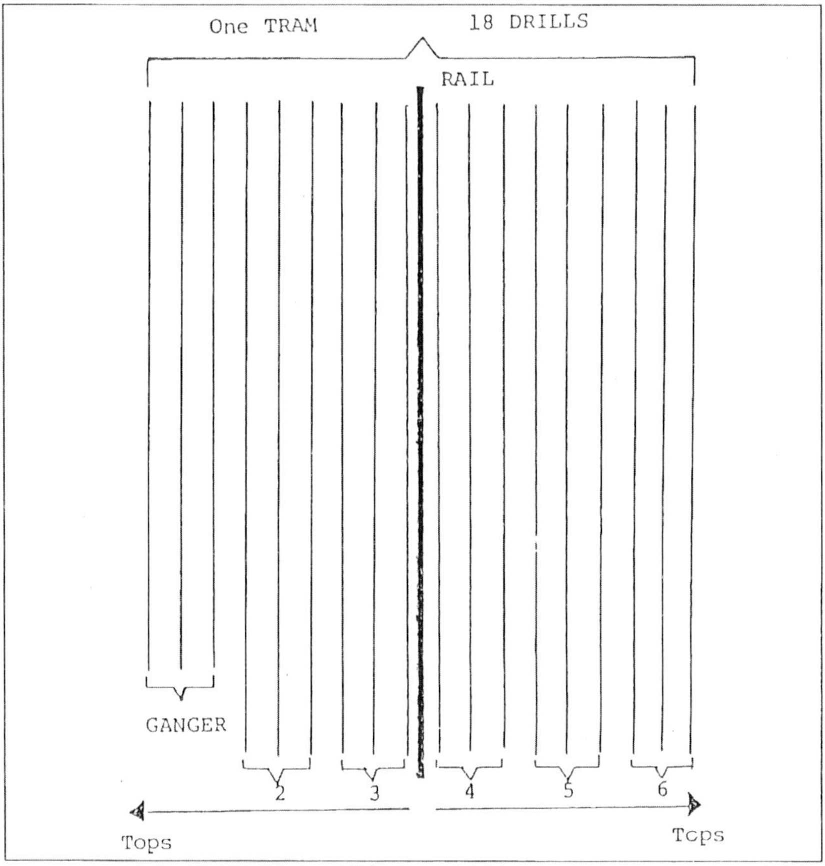

One TRAM
18 DRILLS
RAIL
GANGER
2
3
4
5
6
Tops
Tops

Diagram 4:
Placement of portable rails ready for truck hauling

CUT CANE
CUT CANE
Tops
Tops
Tops
Tops
Tops
Tops
3 drills
3 drills
3 drills
3 drills
3 drills
3 drills
RAIL

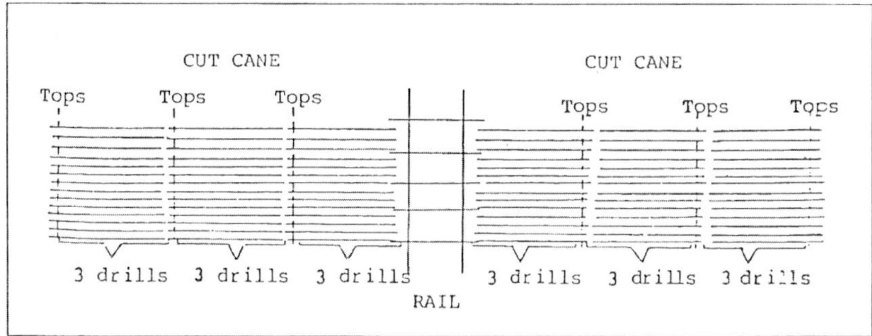

Diagram 5: Position of tops

worked on the handle of their cane knife shortening and/or reducing the size of the grip for comfort. The blade would be sharpened and also bent by the cutter to make it parallel to the ground for a more effective cutting angle.[39] The whole implement weighed about 11 oz. Bending down, the cutter encircled two or three stalks of a cane stool chest high with his left arm.[40] He then cut these stalks with a short sharp motion just above ground level. He threw the stalks forward, or with a back-hand motion, depending on his position, on to the ground to form a regular line of cane in readiness for gathering into bundles for loading.[41]

Topping on the ground came in use in the late 1940s and early 1950s. Rather "hit or miss" compared with the older selective topping - cutting off the leafy top before stalks were laid on the ground -[42] it was much quicker. To be kept razor sharp, cane knives were sharpened frequently by file. In the field the file was often stored in an iron-piping filestick with a tin on top, described as "standing like an erect unrelenting overseer on the headland".[43] Sometimes cutters carried their own files in a self-fashioned holster hanging from their waists. On an average, a cutter would wear out three or four knives in a season. Stones which broke knives on impact, or sandy soil which ground blades down might result in a cutter wearing through up to six knives in a season.[44]

Prolonged rain prevented cutting, but if a burn had just been finished when the rain set in, the gang might choose to cut that block. Though hampered and discomforted by the rain many regarded "three or four tons better than nothing".[45] In *The Cruel Field* Mark "brooded on the two evils: either you got in your burn and worked in the rain till it deafened you - or you missed out and earned sod all!"[46]

Canecutting was a seasonal occupation. The slack season lasted five months of year. As much money as possible had to be earned while the season lasted; all too soon the distant haze of the slack would be tomorrow's uncertain reality.

The season ended with the ganger cutting the last stalk of cane - his prerogative - with dash and ceremony. "The long sweat was over".[47]

39 Yugoslav canecutter V.V., informal discussion 8 October 1984. See also: Naish, *op. cit.*, p.63. For an amusing and detailed account of the importance attached to shaping and sharpening a caneknife to the cutter's satisfaction, see Burrows & Morton, *op. cit.*, pp.47-48.

40 This account, of course, describes a cutter working right-handed.

41 The three drills when cut resembled a continuous carpet of cane the length of the paddock. (Diagram 5). Good long cane so laid was easily gathered into a bundle for loading. Regular methods had to be set aside when cutting short cane, or "lying-down cane": sometimes such cane would be thrown down in bundles ready for loading. After a period cutting such cane, it was not easy to revert to traditional methods with standing cane. Yugoslav canecutter V.V., informal discussion 18 October 1984.

42 Australian canefarmer S.B., informal discussion October 1984.

43 Naish, *op. cit.*, p.32.

44 Yugoslav canecutter V.V., informal discussion 8 October 1984; Burrows and Morton, *op. cit.*, p.48.

45 Yugoslav canecutter D.N., interviewed 28 May 1983.

46 Naish, *op. cit.*, p.65.

47 Donaldson (*et al.*), *Cane!* p.249.

TIGHTENING THE LOAD
Innisfail, 1951

TRUCK LOADED SINGLE-TIER
Mossman, 1955

facing p.68

HAULING OUT LOADED TRUCKS
Ingham area, 1949

HAULING IN EMPTY BINS
Redlynch, outside Cairns, 1950

(Steel bin, used by C.S.R. mills)

facing p.69

CHAPTER 9

The Seasonal Rhythm

'Why the hell does a man come back?' murmured Mark. 'Why?'

'I wonder why myself often enough when the season is young,' said Ruf. 'When you go out into the cold wet mornings of June and July with your bones and cuts all aching and feel that first icy splash of water off the cane on your neck, you wonder why right enough. And when you trudge home in the dusk the horses and cows and the dog in the yard seem puzzled also - look at you like you're barmy. But it passes .... Then later on in the blaze of November and December, when you curse the sunrise and everyone is getting quick to quarrel, and the bees and march flies are stinging you to fury in the ashes and the syrup of the cane - you wonder why, all right. No good thinking of esplanades and the calm pools of the Barrier Reef; that's no escape. So you think back to the good middle months of the season, when you can sling up your ten ton before smoko, and everything is easier, and now and then you can knock off early like we will today. You're still effing and blinding, all right, but not so bitterly: the cane don't rule you and hurt you any more. And when you hack your ten ton for the next day you can go into some crumby town like Nagonda and skite about it round the bar. And afterwards you can sit round the fire with mates who really know you ... yarning ... telling lies .... And that's why jokers come back.'[1]

1 Naish, *The Cruel Field*, p.77.

However heroic the canecutter may have seemed in popular imagination, his life was not the stuff of romance. The reluctant rising before the sun; the night-time twitchings and thrashings of a body spontaneously reliving the agony of the field; the intrepidly coiled carpet snake inhabiting the outhouse and the cold showers from primitive contraptions, all too soon impressed upon Branko the harsh monotony of his new existence.

Before dawn the gang rose, ate breakfast, put together a smoko and cycled, or walked to the field. Once there the morning rake was loaded on the waiting trucks. This task would take two or three hours.[2] Once the cane was loaded the gang would stop for the morning smoko.

After smoko the gang would start up again and cut till about 11 o'clock when they would trudge back to the barracks for lunch, prepared turn about by a member who had knocked off an hour earlier.[3] After a shower the gang would eat and then rest, until one thirty or two o'clock. Cutting would resume until the ganger indicated smoko once again and the gang would rest "now on the rust-coloured earth before the last session of the day's violence".[4] The gang continued to cut till the day began to cool. Then the rail tracks had to be shifted to enable the loading next morning of the day's rake.

On Sunday evening enough cane was burnt for two to three days cutting. On Tuesday and Thursday cane had to be burnt again. Pushing the fire-break and burning the cane sometimes took several hours so the weary cutters often found their way back to the barracks in the dark and once there:

> Someone cooks a meal. Freezing showers wash off some of the soot and sugar sap and mud and blackness that covers the bodies, and we get to bed as soon as possible. Because at 4.30 next morning we get into those cold, dirt stiffened shirts and shorts again for another day.[5]

During the week evenings passed in a blur of weariness and anticipation of the next day's toil; the weekend glimmered enticingly - a respite from the 'violence'.

After the early mornings and the frenetic pace of workdays, many canecutters were eager to rest on a week-end. Some portion of the week-end might be spent cleaning the barracks and washing clothes, activities frequently sprinkled with skylarking and camaraderie. But for some:

> These feelings of restlessness were usual in him. He was always conscious of the tug of the town. Saturday and the unnatural silence over the deserted farm. The sudden change from the violence of the workdays to the utter tranquillity of the weekend always made him feel ill at ease.[6]

On Saturday mornings thus, many, drawn by the bustle of the town and the rowdy jostling at the bar would walk, push-bike, ride their motorbikes, cadge a lift with the

2 Devanny, *By Tropic Sea and Jungle*, p.21. As seen above, not all gangs loaded first thing in the morning.

3 Only, of course, when the gang did not have a full-time cook.

4 Naish, *That Men Should Fear*, p.114.

5 Tyrell, "The Canecutters are at work", p.27.

6 Naish, *The Cruel Field*, p.141.

SMOKO!

Mossman, 1955

Freshwater, 1949

facing p.70

TAKING A BREAK
Redlynch, 1950

Note the waterbags

facing p.71

farmer or catch a railmotor or bus into town. The sight of canecutters waiting to catch a bus on the turns of the road between Cairns and Gordonvale was one of the memories of the canecutting days for one ex-cutter.[7] Leaving the hotels amply lubricated they would sometimes progress to a favourite cafe. Each sugar town had one that was popularly frequented by migrants. Because the managers were usually Europeans, most commonly Italians, the cuisine was reminiscent of that of the cutters' homelands. The food served in such cafes was appetizingly described in the novel *Burnt Sugar:*

> In the Italian eating houses the labourers plunged their teeth into burning veal steaks; masses of spaghetti, garnished with garlic and peas and butter; great hunks of bread; stews of onions; fried batter; boiled beef in vinegar; stewed celery. Mamma Delia's pepper goulash filled the cane-cutters to bursting point.[8]

Within the first season most migrants had purchased a bicycle; many managed to buy a motorbike soon after. Those who did, spoke with fond memories of days spent exploring the scenic delights of North Queensland. Swimming was a favourite pastime. North Queensland, resplendent with sunshine, waterholes and beaches, afforded the canecutters ample opportunity to boat, swim and fish. Along river banks the barracks clung precariously, nestled amidst tropical fecundity. As Branko drifted in his home-made canoe on the river behind his barracks he revisited the rivers of his childhood. Rivers were neutral ground, their waters a soothing balm to weary bodies: a meeting place where gangs from barracks on either bank would gather to while away lazy, sunny Sunday afternoons.[9] Single canecutters often spent their freetime 'looking for girls'. Dances and the movies were popular rendezvous. As well as going to dance halls and movie theatres in the local community, those migrants who worked near Cairns would sometimes go to dances or parties held at the dependants' holding centre.[10] Those cutters with wives residing in the centre would spend the whole weekend there.[11] Many migrants, eager to become fluent in English as soon as possible, spent much of their free time studying the language.[12] One said that "he read a lot. He spent a lot of time learning English by reading comics. He was able to understand words when looking at the pictures. Later in the season he and some other members of the gang joined the local soccer club...."[13]

Soccer, football and tennis were sometimes played by the young cutters. Soccer was a favourite sport amongst Yugoslav migrant canecutters and one at which they

7 Yugoslav canecutter I.U., interviewed 29 May 1983.
8 F.E. Baume, *Burnt Sugar*, Sydney 1934, p.32.
9 Lithuanian canecutter G.Z., interviewed 30 October 1984.
10 Yugoslav canecutter D.N., interviewed 28 May 1983.
11 Polish canecutter K.M., interviewed 9 November 1984.
12 Yugoslav canecutter G.M., questionnaire completed 12 November 1984.
13 Yugoslav canecutter K.B., questionnaire completed early 1982.

excelled.[14] Others had no time for sporting activities because there was "more than enough sporting activity cutting cane".[15] Those who played sport usually resumed it once the season had progressed and the initial weeks of hardening up were over. More sedentary past times were gambling, cards, reading and yarning in the barracks. Jean Devanny noted that strenuous sports and canecutting did not marry well.

> Some gangs have good discussions at smoko-time - politics and so on. Others yarn about racing, tennis, football, barmaids and beer. They back all the winners in the paddock, and on Saturday they go to town, back all the losers .... Some of the very strong young cutters play football in the early years of cutting, but most of them are done for after 10 years.[16]

Occasionally a migrant who liked to hunt might buy a gun as soon as he had some spare money.[17] The hours spent targeting the exotic fauna so strangely different from the game of the 'old country' helped to make the new one more quickly familiar. Leisure times also helped to redress the isolation of barracks life. Acquaintance with Australians made in sporting clubs or dance halls led on occasion to slack season jobs, new careers and marriage. So the weekend would pass, with Sunday always overshadowed by the prospect of the evening's burn and another's week's 'violence' looming. Naish described Saturday as becoming "... a memory as quickly as a football match: no one saw the Sunday dawn. The sun went down and the weekend was over, for they had to burn again that night."[18]

As the days, weeks and week-ends of the season were ordered by a pattern so too were the months of the season. This pattern was in large part, imposed by the progression from winter to summer.

The first months of the season with their cold mornings: damp cane and hardening-up period soon gave way to the 'good months' when the weather was benevolent; the cane burnt well and the cutter was fit. Then the last months set in heralding the humidity and shimmering heat of summer: early rains, weary bodies and fraying tempers. All the while, as "The Gentlemen of the Flashing Blade"[19] slashed their way through the season, shining through the long months "was the day that kept men cutting", the day they finally cut out.[20] On this 'cut out' day as the ganger "with a cry of ecstasy and a great exaggerated slash, ... ended the season" [21] the emotions were of mingled joy and regret; joy that another season of back-breaking work had come to an end with (for most) the hard-earned money safe in the bank; regret because the

14 Two examples being: Yugoslav canecutters K.B., questionnaire completed early 1982 and his friend D.M., not interviewed.

15 Polish canecutter A.S., interviewed 8 November 1984.

16 Devanny, *By Tropic Sea and Jungle*, p.94.

17 Czech canecutter R.C., interviewed 8 March 1985.

18 Naish, *op. cit.*, p.60.

19 *Ibid.*, p.144.

20 Naish, *That Men Should Fear*, p.150.

21 Naish, *The Cruel Field*, p.213.

gang would now break-up, each member going his own way: "... the daring and song and mateship ...."[22] evaporated.

For those who had failed to save their wages, who had gambled, drunk, frittered away their earnings, the slack was an uncertainty to be feared. Naish's character, Mark, dreaded the oncoming slack. On a drunken binge he ended up spending a night lying, wet and cold, in a cane paddock. Searching for somewhere to sleep he thought:

> This ... this ferreting about in the dark, looking for a corner to lie in, he thought hazily, it's like ... it's like the Slack had come, and there was no barracks any more. And then the monstrous ogre of the Slack reared up through his drunkenness. Soon he would be a deadbeat again, an employed rouseabout to be chased off, reported, run in, given the bum's rush.... People were beginning to sense his money was running out. They were becoming careful and sour, as if he was little better than a criminal. Soon he would be seeking food and shelter again, like a dog.[23]

Canecutters earned in the seven months of the season what regular workers earned in twelve. The choice for those who had saved their earnings was to holiday for the five months between seasons, to find odd jobs locally or to travel south following other seasonal labours or to engage in construction work and the like. Some like Mark of *The Cruel Field* regarded slack jobs with disdain:

> He thought about going south like most northerners did: there were good jobs in Sydney, two thousand, and Melbourne, two and a half thousand, miles away;but if they were so damn' good why did the cutters come trekking back every June - did they like blisters or something? A bit over the basic wage, he thought, and a week's journey getting to it: better to lie on a beach near Cairns and wait for the tax rebate to keep you going till the next Crushing.[24]

A good many canecutters were far more ambitious and with long term goals in mind of buying land, or a business, went south every slack. Again, Ruf, a character of *The Cruel Field* inimitably described this annual migration. Being older and single he was not driven by the necessity to fulfil a goal. He would remain in the North for the slack:

> 'What do you plan to do in the Slack, Ruf? Got a job lined up?' 'No, those days are over for me,' he said. I used to be one of those jokers who put down their knives and rushed off south. Chasing peanuts in Kingaroy, wheat on the Downs, and fruit-picking in Victoria.... There's a lot of little worlds when you're young a lot of memories. They're a kind of holiday. But it's not for me any more. No, on the sunny day when we cut out I'll put up my feet here in the north and wait for that glorious Wet....'[25]

22 *Ibid.*

23 *Ibid.*, p.188.

24 *Ibid.*, p.13.

25 *Ibid.*, pp.76-77.

Later in the story he accepted a planting contract. If cutters decided to stay in the district a number would find field work: hoeing, cutting plant cane, feeding a planter, for some part of the slack. If they remained in the barracks the farmer might recruit them to pull out trees in uncleared land or repair and paint the barracks.[26] A popular slack period destination, not too far afield, was the tobacco region of Mareeba, to which many cutters, particularly migrants, returned slack after slack just as they journeyed back to the sugar towns season after season.

Migrant canecutters often tried a wide range of jobs in the slack season. One who claimed to have tried virtually every job available had been ringbarking, constructing dams, working for the Main Roads Department, labouring on the Cooktown-Laura power line, working in meatworks, and a chocolate factory, and driving trucks for an earth moving firm.[27]

Australian sugar growers were informed as the 1948 season drew to a close that the "Commonwealth Employment Service Officials said that plans had been prepared for the immigrants to be formed into a mobile rural pool to ensure continuity of employment in rural occupations."[28] As seen earlier[29] it was a condition of the displaced persons presence in Australia that he did not compete with Australian labour. The slack season in the sugar towns would provide little enough employment opportunities for locals; the Government was not inclined to permit migrants to remain in the sugar districts drawing the unemployment benefit. It was envisaged that a few would be permitted to remain in the district employed in field work, or to return early for that purpose; others would be directed to the fruit farms of Victoria and South Australia where the harvest season of January to April complemented the sugar harvest. Some were dispatched to the south to fill rural job vacancies, but the system operated rather casually.

As long as a migrant was employed during the slack, the government usually did not interfere.[30] One migrant was found work in a local sawmill by the soccer club of which he was a member.[31] Another approached a sawmill himself and obtained a job; invited back for the next slack he ended up working 12 slacks with the same company.[32] In each sugar town there were some concerns in which slack season work was easily found: in Cairns the brewery, one construction firm and a sawmill. Cutters would be directed to them by the employment office, or would approach the businesses direct or be offered work through a contact. Reminded of a migrant's former trade, the

26 Yugoslav canefarmer A.A., interviewed 6 March 1984.

27 Polish canecutter A.S., interviewed 8 November, 1984.

28 "Immigrant Labour in the Sugar Industry", *Australian Sugar Journal*, 15 October 1948, p.401.

29 See Chapter 2 above.

30 Canecutters interviewed had not found the two year contract unduly restrictive. Most indeed had regarded it as informal and unpoliced. Only one described the application to the Department of Immigration by which formal termination of the contract was obtained after the two years. Yugoslav canecutters D.N., interviewed 28 May 1983, J.P., interviewed 31 March 1984.

31 Yugoslav canecutter K.B., questionnaire completed early 1982.

32 Polish canecutter K.M., interviewed 9 November 1984.

CELEBRATING THE WEEKEND
Mossman, 1955

IN TOWN, SATURDAY MORNING AFTER THE FIRST PAY
Cairns, 1949

One of the last big gangs: eight men and a cook

facing p.74

A BICYCLE: THE FIRST PURCHASE
Cairns, 1949

WEEKEND MOTORCYCLING: 1949

District Employment Officer might try to find him a slack season job related to it. Employment officers often showed sympathetic consideration in other ways as well: a migrant whose wife was in the Holding Centre in Cairns was placed with a local baker for one entire slack. He proved so satisfactory that he was offered an apprenticeship, but declined. On the other hand the C.E.S. sometimes tried to place migrants in the jobs most difficult to fill, and one interested in anything but unskilled labouring might be told bluntly that it was "a job for our boys".[33]

To go to Sydney and"do nothing but sleep"[34] - to hibernate right through the slack - was the yearning of some cutters. In the years after completing his two-year contract Branko often felt that way. Still single, relishing freedom of opportunity, the sense of safety and plenty, but bone-weary after the brutal rigour of the season, he longed for rest and aimless distraction.

The cycle of season and slack affected the sugar towns as well: business, social life, the very atmosphere. John Naish wrote of "the timeless derelict atmosphere of the slack",[35] and of town with "a deserted air as if the slack had already come."[36]

33 Polish canecutter A.S., interviewed 8 November 1984.

34 Lithuanian canecutter G.Z., interviewed 30 October 1984.

35 Naish, *That Men Should Fear*, p.149.

36 Naish, *The Cruel Field*, p.224.

CUT OUT DAY

Hambledon, Cairns area, 1949

facing p.76

SLACK SEASON EMPLOYMENT

Elgin Vale Forestry, via Nanango, 1949-50

CHAPTER 10

The Wage Packet

> ... no canecutter of my acquaintance has ever confessed to be a cutter of stalks because of some deeply moving passion for the job, but only because of the high rate of pay involved.[1]

1 C. Morton, "Sugar in North Queensland", *North Australian Monthly*, September 1957, p.43.

In the era being discussed, sugar production operated under an "assignment" system; the farmer was obliged to send his cane to a specific mill, which was bound to accept all cane sent from his assigned land.[2] Since 1929 a Peak Year Scheme had functioned to guard against overproduction.[3] The "Sugar Peak" was reviewed annually in the light of submissions from each mill area, and of changing market conditions. When the sugar Peak was increased, controlled expansion of areas and tonnages would follow throughout the industry. For each farm production levels were set every year, in relation to the fixed "peak",by the Local Cane Prices Board.[4]

Canecutters generally worked under a *piecework system*, i.e.: they contracted to cut a set number of tons in a season and were paid at a fixed rate for each ton cut. In the far northern region, depending on the size of the farms, a gang of up to eight men would sign a contract with one or more farmers in the one area to cut an agreed tonnage. The earnings would be shared equally amongst members.

Wages and conditions were governed by the *State Sugar Award.* One section covered all field workers: field hands, canecutters and, as the industry mechanized, mechanical loader and harvester operators. The award designated three regions: the *Southern* Region comprised all sugar-growing regions south of the Tropic of Capricorn, the *Central*, those between the Tropic and the 20th parallel of south latitude, and the *Northern*, districts north of the 20th parallel.

Piecework rates were different in each region. Northern canecutters received 3d. a ton more than cutters int he Central, and 6d. more than cutters in the Southern Region.[5] Differential rates also existed within regions: cutting in the Mossman area

2 A. Bell, *The Story of the Sugar Industry in Queensland*, Brisbane 1956, p.18.

3 D.S. Simonett, "Sugar Production in North Queensland", *Economic Geography*, Vol. 30 (1954), p.227.

4 For an outline of sugar price trends post-war, see F.D. Gilles, "Sugar", *Economic News*, Vol. 18, No. 10, Oct 1949, pp.1-4.

5 K.S. Mulherin, "Canecutting Awards in the Queensland Sugar Industry", *Quarterly Rev. of Agricultural Economics*, July 1957, p.147.

earned 6d. a ton more than in the rest of the Northern Region.[6] Originally based on green cane yielding 15 tons or more to the acre, these differences remained constant for years.[7]

A deduction of 20% was made for burnt cane before 1953 and a flat rate of 1s.3d. thereafter. The "cutting" rate covered loading as well; where cane was loaded mechanically the cutter lost 2s.5d. a ton in 1948,[8] rising to 4s.2d. in 1955.[9]

The Sugar Industry Award was administered by the State Industrial Court, whose primary function was to fix the State basic wage. Rates of pay for sugar workers varied with the basic wage, but could also be affected by appeals to the Court by the relevant union - for canecutters, the A.W.U., or by the Queensland Canegrowers Council and the Australian Sugar Producers' Association on behalf of canefarmers.[10]

These rates applied to fields carrying 15 tons to the acre or more. The rate increased in proportion as tonnage fell below that figure; in 1948 a field carrying only five or six tons an acre would earn the cutter up to 20/8 a ton.[11]

6 *Ibid.*, p.148. While drawing heavily upon Mulherin, I have ignored his account of day-labour rates which in practice did not apply to canecutters.

7 The three districts were first defined in 1901 with reference to a bounty paid on cane grown with white labour, which already commanded higher wages in the more northerly districts: 26-1/2% higher than at Bundaberg. (A. Birch, "Organisation and Economics of Pacific Island Labour", *Bus. Archives & History*, Feb. 1968, p.73, and "The Magic Grass", *People*, 18 February 1858, p.36). This was a function partly of scarcity, partly of adverse working conditions. Higher rainfall in the north had results which adversely affected cutting rates: (a) heavier, more tangled cane (a problem progressively eliminated by selective breeding of cane varieties);(b) more frequent interruptions to harvesting; and (c) higher humidity, making work more uncomfortable. Australian canefarmer S.B., discussion 22 October 1984.

8 Sugar Industry State Award: Canecutting Wages & Conditions, *Q. Industrial Gazette*, 30 June 1948, p.692.

9 State Award Variation, *Ibid.*, 30 June 1955.

10 Mulherin, *op. cit.*, p.148.

11 State Award, *Q. Industrial Gazette*, 30 June 1948, p.692.

TABLE 10.3

MOVEMENTS IN STATE BASIC WAGE AND CANECUTTING AWARD IN THE QUEENSLAND SUGAR INDUSTRY: NORTHERN ZONE[12]

DATE OF OPERATION	BASIC WAGE (per week)			PIECEWORK CUTTING RATE (per ton)		WEEKLY EARNINGS OF AN AVERAGE CUTTER		
	£	s.	d.	s.	d.	£	s.	d
1948								
1 January	5	19	0	9	0	15	15	0
2 February	6	1	0	9	1	15	17	11
26 April	6	4	0	9	2½	16	2	3½
17 May	6	4	0	10	4	18	1	8
2 August	6	7	0	10	5½	18	6	0½
1 November	6	9	0	10	6½	18	8	1½
1949								
31 January	6	12	0	10	7	18	10	5
2 May	6	13	0	10	8½	18	14	9½
1 August	6	16	0	10	10	18	19	2
31 October	6	19	0	10	11½	19	3	6½
1950								
30 January	7	1	0	11	0½	19	6	5½
1 May	7	3	0	11	1½	19	9	4½
31 July	7	6	0	11	3	19	13	9
30 October	7	9	0	11	4½	19	18	1½
7 December	8	4	0	12	0	21	0	0
1951								
5 February	8	9	0	12	2½	21	7	3½
30 April	8	16	0	12	6	21	17	6
30 July	9	5	0	12	10½	22	10	7½
29 October	9	15	0	13	3½	23	5	2½
3 December	9	15	0	13	3½	23	5	2½

12 Adapted from Mulherin, *op. cit.*, pp.150-151; third column calculated with the aid of Australian canefarmer S.B.

It will be seen from the Table that in November 1948 an average canecutter in good cane was earning nearly three times, and in December 1951 just under two and a half times, the basic wage.[13] At the rate of seven tons a day the average cutter cut about 35 tons a week: about 1000 tons in a season of roughly 28 weeks. His earnings in 1951, the rate per ton averaging 12s.10d., were about £641.13.4 for the seven month season.

Cutting rates like these were well above those reported from other sugar-producing countries, as was often remarked at the time.Explanations offered included payment at piecework rates, contracts by which gangs agreed to deliver a stipulated minimum tonnage per day, and the gang system of sharing earnings equally.[14] This seems reasonable.

At first migrant cutters made less than the basic wage, but as their efficiency increased they could earn more than twice that amount.[15] One who got out after his two contract years said it paid well: he "saved £1000 over two years. It was quite comparable or better than any job but it had no future."[16] On the other hand, a Lithuanian who made good money in his first season saved only forty or fifty pounds: typical, he said of his compatriots' attitude towards money.[17]

To compensate for the seasonal nature of the canecutting employ a loading provision was incorporated into the Award. Having been about 7s.6d. per week it rose by 5s. in 1951, and rose marginally once again in that year.[18] From the earnings of a piecework canecutter 6d. per ton was withheld by the farmer as "retention money". Canecutters contracted on sign-on day to cut a prescribed tonnage of cane for a canefarmer; retention money was devised to hold men to their contract. The money was to be banked and at the completion of the contract the sum of retained money plus accrued interest was to be paid to the canecutter. Clive Morton stated repeatedly that the retention money was little incentive for canecutters to honour their contracts and that in fact canecutters took their contracts lightly. The cutters he observed:

> ... flit through to some other mill area, stop there for a few weeks and start on the merry-go-round again. In most cases they do not get summoned for breach of contract because the police are far from keen to look for them if they are not in their own police area at the time the summons is

13 At 15 or more tons to the acre, he was cutting 1/4 to 1/2 an acre a day.

14 A.B. Henderson, "Output of Australian Cane Cutters" in *The Australian Sugar Journal*, 19 March 1961, p.1006.

15 Polish canecutter K.M., interviewed 9 November 1984. The wage was then about £14 a fortnight.

16 Yugoslav canecutter and canefarmer M.M., interviewed 21 October 1984.

17 Lithuanian canecutter G.Z., interviewed 30 October 1984.

18 Mulherin, *op. cit.*, p.151.

> prepared. Let any mill area dare to openly refuse to sign-on these noted flitters, and the union cry of 'victimisation' would echo to the ceiling.[19]

In direct contrast is John Naish's Jeff who was proud and honourable in the extreme. Despite debilitating illness he was determined to cut till the end of season in order to claim his retention money. As he saw it, "losing retention money was the symbol and the result of quitting."[20]

Most canecutters reneged on a contract at one time or another. Few would do so as flippantly and wilfully as Clive Morton described, or place such frantic importance on the retention money as depicted by John Naish. For cases like 'Jeff' who was too ill to complete the contract, the State Award stipulated that on presentation of a medical certificate the full amount deducted be paid to the canecutter.[21]

If a canecutter did not complete his contract for any other reason - leaving for another cut, finding the job too difficult, or leaving for a slack season job before 'cut out' day - he forfeited his retention money which was distributed to the other members of the gang at the completion of the contract. If the whole gang reneged and thereby forfeited its retention money the State Award prescribed for the farmer the action to be taken. Usually the money was paid to the replacement gang. Sometimes a very unsatisfactory gang or gang member would be asked to forfeit the contract. Then the farmer would pay over the retention money for the sake of industrial harmony.

A gang which had fulfilled its contract could still lose some of its retention money if the mill docked the farmer for "dirty" (i.e. inadequately topped) cane or for overloaded trucks. Topping on the ground and mechanical loading were often blamed for dirty cane. The penalty would be anything between £2 and £20 per truck,[22], half of which the farmer was entitled to recover from retention money. Disputes over non-payment or underpayment of retention money went for arbitration by the Industrial Magistrate whose ruling was final.

Rates higher or lower than the standard figure could be set in a number of specified circumstances. Cutters could demand a higher rate for a paddock littered with stones or infested with sensitive weed or for cane stunted, rat-eaten or storm-tangled; all made cutting more hazardous or difficult.

When a gang was dissatisfied with the state of the field or the cane the ganger would inform the farmer that the normal rate was insufficient. If the gang were very militant, or on bad terms with the farmer, they would down tools while the farmer summoned

19 C. Morton, "'Dry-cleaned' cane is not clean enough", *North Australian Monthly*, September 1958, p.49. Proceedings for breach of contract were certainly taken on occasion. "In the Cairns district trouble was experienced with new Australian gangs and prosecutions were taken against offenders. Although the matters ended with a withdrawal of the prosecutions on terms favourable to employers, there is no doubt that the proceedings impressed the cutters in question with a respect for our industrial code." *The Producers' Review*, 5 April 1950.

20 Naish, *The Cruel Field*, pp.116-11.

21 *Q. Industrial Gazette*, 30 June 1948, p.693.

22 C. Morton, "Crushing Comment", *North Australian Monthly*, Sept 1957, p.43; R. Boland, "A 'Fair Go' for the Cane Cocky", *Ibid.*, May 1959, pp.9-10.

the Cane Inspector. After examining the conditions complained of, the Cane Inspector would propose an appropriate rate. If the gang rejected it the A.W.U. representative was called in to negotiate with the Cane Inspector. If they could not agree the Industrial Magistrate was sent for: the rate he determined was final.[23]

More commonly the farmer would suggest a rate. This the gang might find acceptable, conscious that some considerable time might elapse before the Cane Inspector turned up, time during which no cane would be cut and no money earned. Even if the Cane Inspector was sent for, the ganger and the farmer might have reached agreement on the rate by the time he arrived, for there was no telling who would benefit by waiting for his decision.[24] However determined, the special rate would be recorded by the mill.

A higher rate could be obtained in some other circumstances; one arose quite commonly at the end of the season. Cutters who had completed their contracts could get additional work as a "fly" gang: one directed by a Cane Inspector to another farm, whether in the same area or in another district, to help out a gang running behind its contract, or a farmer deserted by cutters who had gone off to slack jobs. There was often competition for such work. Desperate to have his cane cut before the season closed, and aware of the scarcity of cutters still available, a farmer could be dragooned into paying as much as £1 a ton.[25] A fly gang might earn between £100 and £120 a fortnight.[26]

The 1954 season was one in which special circumstances prevailed. Labour was scarce because migrants under contract to cut cane for the first time proved unsuitable and deserted their contracts. To exacerbate the situation, the season's crop was a large one and crushing ran behind schedule because of unseasonal heavy rainfalls. It was reported by the A.S.P.A. that "many canecutters shamelessly exploited the worries and anxieties of the growers by refusing to continue their contracts except at exorbitant piecework rates."[27] But they were not the only ones at fault:

> ... some growers, very concerned at the problem of getting suitable labour, enticed cutters away from their contracts by offering higher rates.... These factors led to chaotic labour conditions in some northern mill areas; very exorbitant cutting rates were paid in some areas in the later stage of the season, and these bore very heavily upon the farmers affected.[28]

Understandably, the farmers were exhorted to:

> ... stand firm and united against any repetition of cutters' efforts to enforce exorbitant rates of pay, and ... completely support the established proce-

23 *Q. Industrial Gazette*, 30 June 1948, p.692.

24 Yugoslav canefarmer M.G., interviewed 1 April 1984.

25 Yugoslav canefarmer M.G., interviewed 1 April 1984, and Yugoslav canecutter D.N., interviewed 18 May 1983.

26 Russian canecutter B.I., interviewed 7 November 1984, Polish canecutter A.S., interviewed 8 November 1984, Yugoslav canecutter V.V., informal discussion 8 October 1984.

27 A.S.P.A. *Annual Report*, 1955, p.6.

28 *Ibid.*

dure for fixation of rates in special circumstances, namely by decision of the Cane Inspector subject to appeal to the Industrial magistrate.[29]

As discussed earlier, for many migrant cutters the normal 'hardening-up' pains were accentuated by the fact that their bodies were totally unaccustomed to hard work. They may have found the work considerably more difficult and laborious than other new-chum cutters. Moreover they were often cutting cane that experienced gangs 'wouldn't touch'. Two displaced person cutters recalled that their first contracts were to farmers who had lost their first gang or who could not find another willing to take on the contract because their fields were full of stones.

Some farmers may have asked for a migrant gang knowing that it would not be aware of having entered into a bad contract, and bound by the two-year agreement to fulfil the contract even when it did wake up.[30] One migrant recalled of his first season that "if they knew anything about cane they would not have stayed" on their first farm.[31]

Though a 44 hour working week was operative when the first of the displaced persons arrived, a 40 hour week was introduced in 1948. The canecutter could work his eight hour day anytime between 6 a.m. and 6 p.m. Strict policing of work outside these hours was attempted by the A.W.U. organiser, but with limited effect on outlying farms. Some gangs would extend their cutting time by starting to load at 4.30 a.m. Infrequently - usually only to take a week day off for some special reason - a gang would rise soon after midnight, do a day's work by the light of hurricane lamps, and down tools as morning broke.[32] Similarly, for their own benefit, or at the request of the farmer, they might harvest on a week-end. This was done surreptitiously by cutting from the centre of the tram. From outside the tram looked untouched, while in fact a square of cane at the centre had been harvested.[33] Offenders apprehended by the A.W.U. Organizer had to 'show cause' before the Industrial magistrate and could be fined as much as £10 or £20 a head.

A 'State of Emergency' could be declared for individual farmers or mill areas with the Industrial Magistrate's cognizance if labour shortages or adverse weather threatened to extend the season unduly. Canecutters could then work overtime, on weekends and even on statutory holidays. For each hour's overtime worked on a weekday or Saturday the cutter received half the hourly wage on top of the normal piecework rate, and the full hourly wage on top of the piecework rate for each hour worked on a Sunday.[34] Cutting on statutory holidays earned double the piecework rate.[35]

29 *Ibid.*

30 Russian canecutter B.I., interviewed 6 November 1984.

31 Yugoslav canecutter K.B., questionnaire completed early 1982.

32 Yugoslav canecutter and cane farmer M.M., interviewed 21 October 1984.

33 *Ibid.*; Yugoslav canecutter V.V., informal discussion 8 October 1984.

34 "Canecutters Working Overtime", *Producers' Review*, 15 July 1950, p.47

35 A.S.P.A. *Annual Report*, 1955, p.6.

The canecutter was paid fortnightly. The hours worked by each gang member were recorded by the ganger in a time-book, which was handed to the farmer each fortnight. He computed the fortnight's pay for each gang member in relation to the work recorded in the time-book and the mill weights of the fortnight's tonnage cut. The farmer could be fined if such a book was not kept.[36]

Farmers made use of private accountants or the local Cane Growers' Executive to make up their cutters' pay-packets which were usually brought to the paddock or barracks on the Friday afternoon. Two farmers in the Mossman district recall that there, a Cane Growers' Executive representative was accompanied by a policeman when he brought the pay-packets to the field on Friday afternoon.[37] Elsewhere the farmer simply distributed the pay-packets himself at the barracks.[38]

"Money was understood pretty quickly by migrants"[39] and certainly it does seem to have been a major preoccupation. One of a Czech gang that split up four months into its first season said that the main reason was unhappiness with the money they were earning. And even when a migrant had an opportunity to improve his occupational status he often declined in order to return to canecutting. One such migrant worked in a bakery for his first slack. He was offered but did not take an apprenticeship because as he put it, he had "sugar in the blood": the money he had been earning by the end of the season was more than he would have made in the bakery.[40]

Similar tales abound. Canecutting enabled the migrant to acquire material goods that he would not necessarily have been able to purchase on wages. A Polish canecutter returning from a spell in Victoria, was offered a job at the Sugar Terminal; he asked to be allowed two seasons canecutting to accumulate the deposit on a house before taking it up.[41] Another Polish cutter went back to cutting each season in part for the things he could buy: a car and a house.[42] Those who gave up to go share farming in tobacco or to work in the timber industry and failed to make good often returned to canecutting to get back on their feet.[43]

The system of paying canecutters had built-in potential for friction. Growers begrudged parting with their money; cutters felt under paid for their hard work. Writings on the industry tend to depict relations between farmers and cutters as chronically strained. Curlewis[44] referred to "the inordinate and unreasonable demands of labour" which forced millers and growers into co-operative organizations.[45] Clive Morton [46] gives colourful details of avaricious cutters cornering the

36 *Q. Industrial Gazette*, 30 June 1950, pp.692-4.

37 Yugoslav canefarmers M.G. and A.A., interviewed 1 April 1984 and 6 March 1983.

38 Australian canefarmer S.B., informal discussion 1984.

39 Yugoslav canecutter and canefarmer M.M., interviewed 21 October 1984.

40 Yugoslav canecutter J.P., interviewed 31 March 1984.

41 Polish canecutter A.S., interviewed 8 March 1984.

42 Polish canecutter K.M., interviewed 9 November 1984.

43 Yugoslav canecutters M.L., interviewed 15 May 1983 and J.P., interviewed 31 April 1984. Also Polish canecutter: A.S., interviewed 8 November 1984.

44 F.C.P. Curlewis, *An Aspect of the Australian Sugar Industry*, 1933, p.6.

45 The Australian Sugar Producers' Association Limited and The Queensland Canegrowers' Council.

46 C. Morton, "Sugar in North Queensland", *North Australian Monthly*, Jan 1956, p.47.

"worried, harassed and desperate" farmer, compromising him with "stand over tactics". Without a doubt animosity did arise from the canecutters' demands for a better price and the farmers' reluctance to meet them. In conversation between Mark and Ruf, John Naish revealed the ill-feeling that arguments over price could generate between gang members. The conversation was initiated by Mark who,surveying a field after a storm, observed that:

> This was the snag with canecutting. Some years there was hardly a stick out of place; but others, when the wet and wind got together, whole paddocks of cane fell lodged and twisted and rotting on the earth, twice as slow to harvest, twice as backbreaking.
>
> ... 'if the cane's down, no messing about: you hit up that bastard Peter for a price!'
>
> 'I don't love the man' said Ruf, calmly but almost coldly, 'and I don't work for nothing.' Into the silence came the first whiff of the dissension that clouded the canefields in the bad years: dispute welling up now and then into trouble and violence, bane of the arbiters. The cane-harvest grossed millions: the carve up was sometimes vicious enough when the knives stopped slashing in the sun.[47]

But the canecutter was not always at fault nor the canefarmer blameless. The season of 1954[48] was a case in point: the farmers 'stole' canecutters from their legitimate contracts. In *The Cruel Field* the farmer bribed the Cane Inspector to hand down a pre-arranged rate for bad cane; the cutters accepted, though it was unfair as the farmer's brother told him:

> 'Iss not fair price, Peter. Magistrate would give them more.'
>
> 'The more fools them: they didn't get him!'
>
> 'Peter,' said Tony, uncomfortably, '... I hope you no give Meester Forrester money.' But Peter was quietly watching the toiling cutters, as if in a world of his own making. 'Bend your backs, you dogs!' he said grimly. 'Chip, chop, chip, chop you'll lose a drop of sweat there at twelve bob a ton!'[49]

The special rate allowed for bad cane was to compensate for the slower pace of cutting. Often the farmer would help out himself in such cases. Not so Peter: whereas most farmers "were discreet enough to disappear when the cane was as grim as this, disappear or get a knife and hop into it, ... Peter was still leaning on a hoe enjoying their struggles - gloating ...."[50] Under such conditions dissension between farmer and canecutter was not surprising.

Yet at bottom the real interests of cutter and grower were not in conflict: each wanted to get the cane out of the paddock as quickly and cleanly as possible. A gang operated at its best when all members were in accord. The tensions resulting from a

47 Naish, *op. cit.*, p.16.
48 See above, p.82-3.
49 Naish, *op.cit.*, p.37.
50 Naish, *op. cit.*, p.199.

farmer's attempt at exploitation could engender intra-gang strife and impair efficiency. Thus a farmer who treated his cutters fairly and kept on good terms with them enhanced his own prospects for a trouble-free prosperous season.

The term commonly used for the cane farmer was 'cocky'.[51] Faintly disparaging in tone it appears frequently in canecutting literature. In Bill Scott's poem "The last of the Hand Cutters" there is reference both to the 'cocky' and to the old animosity between cutter and 'cocky':

In the lounge at the White Horse one Saturday night ....
The rain belted down on the pavement outside
When an old drunk climbed up on a table and cried -

'Farewell to days of the file and the knife....

'I've cut down at Childers where the cockys are mean,
They grizzle and moan if you don't top it clean. ....

Then he fell from the table and flat on the floor
When a cocky there present let out this loud roar -

'Oh die, you old bastard and stop your complaining!'
So he snuffed it. Outside the rain just kept on raining....[52]

Dan Sheahan in his poem "The Cane Harvest" was a little kinder, depicting the 'cocky' as much wronged as the cutter:

When harvest days are ended
—and dark clouds hide the hills -
On a great deck chair extended
The farmer views his bills.

His 'Cocky' blood is boiling
While paying every debt -
To those that did the toiling
And them that never sweat.

He holds a cheque book cover
With one leaf in the butt -
And that won't be left over

51 A generic term for farmers, especially small farmers, throughout Australia for fully a century. E. Partridge, *Dictionary of Slang*.

52 For the full version see Scott, *Complete Book of Australian Folklore*, pp.334-335.

> When Sir Artie gets his cut.[53]

> Blatant exploitation of migrant cutters on the farms seems to have been uncommon; it was sometimes tried by shopkeepers who would claim that the gang owed more than the real amount.[54] But migrants were aware of the risk of being duped when shopping. One Lithuanian migrant going to town to buy a watch - often the first purchase, eagerly anticipated, took with him an Australian friend to make sure he was not "tricked".[55] Sadly, migrants more often experienced exploitation by their own countrymen. A Yugoslav farmer and wife who preferred to employ their own countrymen are reputed to have said frequently "... now it is our turn."[56] The implication was that by exploiting ignorant migrants now they could compensate for the time they had suffered, scrimped and saved when they first migrated. The avaricious Italian canefarmer of *The Cruel Field* hinted at the same possibilities:

> The Australian was a devil for his five minutes' blow that became ten-fifteen if you didn't watch it - but you'd be the worst man alive if you ever docked a shilling from his pay! They'd had their own way too long. It was time the growers chartered a ship of their own and dumped ten thousand Napoli unemployed on the canefields: the Minister for Immigration was too slow, too slow, it needed doing now, quickly.[57]

While some farmers may have wished to exploit their canecutters there was a limit to the means they could adopt. Theoretically they should not have been able to underpay them. Displaced persons were brought into the country under the condition that they would be employed at the same rate of pay as Australian workers. While the migrant was under contract the C.E.S. could monitor that he was not being paid beneath the going rate. As for the canecutter, the local Cane Growers' Executive, through which most canecutters' wages were transacted, carefully scrutinized employment details submitted to them so as to guard against underpayment. Initially, a farmer could keep the canecutter ignorant of the recourse he had when cane was 'bad', and of the protection his Union offered. However a migrant's ignorance was soon dispelled once he had mastered some English and socialized with canecutters of other gangs. A farmer could house the migrant canecutters in a sub-standard barracks, but only at the risk of being prosecuted for breach of *The Workers' Accommodation Act*. Where relations with the farmer were good a gang might stay on for years. The state of the cane and of the fields, together with the farmer's attitude, determined whether the

53 D. Sheahan, *Songs from the Canefields*, pp.116-117. Sir Arthur ("Artie") Fadden was Federal Treasurer from 1949 to 1957.

54 Yugoslav canecutter and canefarmer M.M., interviewed 21 October 1984.

55 Lithuanian canecutter G.Z., interviewed 30 October 1984.

56 Yugoslav canecutter (wife) M.L., interviewed 15 May 1983.

57 Naish, *op. cit.*, p.155.

gang would stay on or seek a new contract the next season. For this reason also it was in the farmer's own interest to treat his gang fairly and look after its welfare. Many heart-warming tales survive of farmers going out of their way to be helpful.[58]

Farming any crop is precarious: so much depends on the capricious forces of nature, on unpredictable fluctuations of demand and the changing circumstances of the national and international political and economic climates. Sugar was a labour intensive crop, cultivated in tropical conditions where labour was always difficult to secure and hold. The farmer resented the demands pressed by labour because, though not driven by the same urgency, he was motivated by the same goal: money. He considered his money hard won when the precariousness of sugar farming was taken into account. This produced the real and the recounted conflict between cutter and 'cocky'.

58 Polish canecutter K.M., interviewed 9 November 1984; Czech canecutter R.C., interviewed 8 March 1985; Yugoslav canecutter I.D., interviewed 5 November 1984.

CHAPTER 11

'Why the hell does a man come back?'

"And when you hack your ten ton for the next day you can go into some crumby town like Nagonda and skite about it round the bar. And afterwards you can sit round the fire with mates who really know you ... yarning ... telling lies. ... And that's why jokers come back."[1]

1 Naish, *The Cruel Field*, p.77.

High earnings did not attract many newcomers into canecutting, especially in the northern region, in the years of full employment that followed the Second World War. Certainly there seemed to be little else to attract them; "the job itself is monotonous, dirty, hard and demanding."[2] Why, then, did migrants continue cutting years after their commitment to the Commonwealth had been met?[3] For some, the money together with the nature of contract work provide the explanation; as Mark put it in *The Cruel Field*:

> Fifty or sixty bob a day planting was no good to him,for canecutting would soon bring him in twice that much: he needed work where a man could save some dough, not merely mark time. Besides the less an employer paid you, the more you were *bossed* - and the more he thought he was doing you a favour: wages jobs were for born serfs. Thank God canecutting was contract work, and the cutter was the contractor: he signed on at the mill to take off the crop, and the less interference the better.[4]

For most, it seems, it was the life itself:

> It was people without trade or profession [who] made sugar their business.... it was certain type of man that made canecutters. Perhaps it was the comradeship, the competition like a sport and the money that kept them going.[5]

Though the work was tougher, harder "than working one mile underground in a coalmine in Russia",[6] it became for some a way of life, given up with real regret.

> With the last season he felt funny. One job disappeared forever. He always thought about cane. It was fun when the season came even though canecutting was hard work. He really liked canecutting.[7]

So it was for Branko. Over the years he held many interesting and well-paid slack jobs, but none held for him the blend of attractions in canecutting. Marriage did not alter this. He met his wife at a picnic outing on the banks of the Barron River. Gentle, quietly spoken, with an aura of imperturbable calm she roused vague and disturbing memories of his aunt. A music teacher, she taught at her parents' home pupils usually indifferent and seldom dexterous. Marriage followed a brief and fervent courtship. Branko was 35. His wife, born and bred in Cairns, had hoped to live near her ageing parents. With some compromise they purchased a small plot of land outside Cairns and built with pride and hope a typically '50's style of fibrolite house. They settled into married life and awaited longingly the children that never ensued. Branko continued

2 Yugoslav canecutter K.B., questionnaire completed early 1982.
3 See Table 2, Chapter 4, above.
4 Naish, *op. cit.*, p.14.
5 Yugoslav canecutter V.V., written comunication, early 1982.
6 Yugoslav canecutter J.P., interviewed 31 Mar 1984, quoting another migrant.
7 Polish Canecutter K.M., interviewed 9 Nov 1984.

to cut, sometimes now attacking the cane with pent-up anger. His wife kept house and played tender and increasingly more wistful music, heard only by the occasional tree snake and the willy wagtails and mynah birds competing for melodic honours.

More commonly canecutters gave up on getting married, feeling that the seasonal upheaval was not for wife and children, who were entitled to the security of a settled home. One Yugoslav simply "could not envisage spending his [married] life in barracks and moving from season to season to another location."[8]

Those who remained in the industry expected and received substantial remuneration for their labour. Canecutters' wages were a major cost for the industry: 25% of the total cost of production in 1954-5.[9] That fact, together with the dwindling supply of cutters, made inevitable the development of a more efficient method of harvesting the Australian sugar crop.

Just 20 years after the first of the displaced persons walked onto the North Queensland canefields 72% of the Queensland sugar crop was being mechanically harvested:[10] two years later, 92%.[11] In December 1977 all reference to manual canecutters was deleted from the Sugar Industry Award.

Burrows and Morton assert that "The canecutters themselves took their fate surprisingly calmly with most reconciled to mechanization."[12] Australia was still enjoying buoyant years of full employment when those still cutting in the late 1960s and early 1970s found themselves in search of new work. They could be confident of finding other employment relatively easily with their proven penchant for hard work, their work ethics of commitment to a group goal and faithfulness to a contract.

Those displaced persons who like Branko cut into the sunset days of manual harvesting were themselves entering the twilight years of their working lives. Though the more astute may have foreseen the inevitable as early as the later 1950s, it was not simply mechanization that drove them from the field, but advancing age coupled with the timely availability of other jobs.

Branko had worked each slack with the local council for some years. When in 1969 he was offered permanent employment he accepted with little regret. His new career had a lot to recommend it. It was secure until retirement; it was far less physically demanding than cutting and entailed tending gardens, a task he enjoyed.

Formerly by June each year, sugar towns from Mossman to Rocky Point had reverberated with anticipation of the forthcoming sugar harvest and the arrival of the canecutters. Mark, a character in *The Cruel Field* observed this as:

8 Yugoslav canecutter K.B., questionnaire completed early 1982. Yugoslav canecutter and canefarmer M.M., interviewed 21 Oct 1984, married at the end of his two years contract and left canecutting behind.

9 This compared with "16% for all hired labour in the wheat industry in the same season and 19% for dried vine fruit." Mulherin, "Canecutting Awards, p.152.

10 For a comprehensive and interesting account of mechanical cane harvesters and their displacing the manual canecutter, see Burrows and Morton, *The Canecutters*.

11 *Ibid.*, p.187.

12 *Ibid.*, p.242.

> He gazed down on the stirring town, which was daily becoming more charged with expectancy as the crushing season approached. There had been the trickle of canecutters and millworkers off the southern mail train for some weeks past: trade was getting brisker in the pubs and stores and boarding houses.[13]

In the novel *Cane!* there is a very explicit description of the significance of the canecutters' remigration to a small sugar town: Innisfail. Simultaneously the sketch drew attention to the spare time inclinations of the canecutter:

> The long sleep is over. Storekeepers have restacked their shelves, publicans have filled their cellars and tightened the screws on bar-rails and doors. In the boarding houses freshly patched sheets cover old mattresses, spiders and cockroaches have been routed, ant-holes blocked, and clean glass ashtrays decorate the dressing tables. Even the windows have been polished so you can see what goes on the other side without spitting and rubbing hard with your elbow. The bootmaker stands in his doorway, squinting down the long road to the station, licking his lips and juggling the small ancient coin in his pocket that is his luck-piece. Sam Batten can smell money on the other side of a ten foot wall. Along Down Street the girls are naked in their rooms, having a last look at their working clothes. Innisfail is ready.[14]

The introduction of the mechanical harvester marked more than the demise of outmoded skills. Of greater significance was the loss to the towns of the "... exhilarating climate of the annual crushing season," the overt prosperity of the season when "Farmers, cutters, business and professional men, all sections of the community basked in the sun of the crushing boom."[15]

The word 'overt' is used because it would be grossly incorrect to say that the passing of the manual canecutter wreaked financial doom on the sugar communities. In reality, mechanical harvesting meant that the profits were distributed amongst fewer hands. In addition, whereas the canecutter was likely to take his money elsewhere at the end of the season, harvesting became the province of the farmers themselves or of local harvestor contractors; the money generated by the harvest stayed in the community. The real significance to the town of the sugar season in the days of the canecutter was not in matter but in atmosphere.[16]

No longer did sugar towns prepare for the annual onslaught; no longer were picture houses packed with canecutters on a Saturday night; no more did young women look forward to the frequent dances in the 'Shire Hall' that the presence of so many single young men made possible. The deserted air of an eternal slack settled on the towns.

13 Naish, *op. cit.*, p.12.

14 Donaldson, (*et al.*)*Cane!*, pp.42-43.

15 Gollschewsky, "The Yesterdays and Todays of the Sugar Cane Industry", p.75.

16 L. Roberts, "What mechanization will mean to the North", *North Australian Monthly*, July 1959, p.41.

CONCLUSION

... displaced persons adapted themselves to the severity of the work and climate on harvesting sugar last season [1948] .... Between sugar seasons, nearly one hundred of the cutters have been accommodated by the Commonwealth in Melbourne, and employed at the sugar refinery. As a result, all sugar necessary for processing the last fruit harvest was available, and once again, after years of shortage, white sugar is becoming plentiful in Victoria. The housewife who now can buy white sugar instead of having to make do with raw sugar can thank the Displaced Persons Scheme, because here, as in many other industries, the main labour force of Australians, while providing the bulk of the output, is not enough to make up the small margin which changes the supply position from one of crippling shortage to one of sufficiency or near-sufficiency.[1]

1 Conference of Commonwealth & State Ministers on Immigration, 16 May 1949. AA: CRS A445, 1949-; 145/3/7 pt 2.

The days of the manual canecutter are long since over. Years ago displaced persons discarded their clumsy tag 'New Australian' and merged into the mosaic of Australian society. For most, their immediate legacy is modest: offspring, and a wealth of stories and memories for anyone who cares to listen. Nevertheless as canecutters and as displaced persons these men are of enormous significance in North Queensland history.

The displaced persons arrived in Australia at a time when, for numerous reasons, migration without parallel was acceptable to the general populace. The Government organisation catering for their reception, dispersion and employment ensured that neither trade unions nor ordinary Australian workers felt threatened: itself a remarkable achievement. They were directed to occupations which unskilled workers could avoid in that era of full employment, and bound to them by two-year contracts. Generally they accepted the employment allocated, and the contracts, good-humoredly, as just repayment for their fares to freedom and safety.

Within the sugar industry their contribution was warmly acknowledged.

> The work they have gone to has frequently been difficult. In every case it has been heavy work for which Australian labour was not offering or was in short supply. In the case of the sugar cane cutters, the work was something quite new to the migrants. But they entered the canefields with enthusiasm, and reports from the cane-growers attest to the fine work they have performed.[2]

The character and scale of the preparation made by the Australian Government for the reception of displaced persons between 1947 and 1951 was itself unprecedented in the history of migration to Australia. The initial propaganda to make the scheme palatable to the public; arrangements for recruitment and screening in Europe; the registering and listing of successful applicants and dependants; the disembarkation procedure and processing; the initial housing and feeding; distribution of civilian clothing and work clothing in specific instances; monetary allowances and Alien Registration papers; entertaining; language education; placing in, and transporting to employment; care of dependants in holding centres; maintaining of records of whereabouts over the two year contract period: all was planned with remarkable detail and precision.

The two year contract was not unique for it was used in administering other contemporary and later migration schemes: the migration of former Polish soldiers, Italians for work in the N.S.W. and Queensland sugar fields, and refugees arriving under the I.C.E.M. scheme. What was original was the impact of displaced persons bound by a two year contract upon the whole Australian sugar industry. Prior to their arrival and even as only trickles of these migrants reached the sugar districts in the years 1948 to 1951, they were hailed as redeemers of a faltering industry.[3] The displaced person as contracted sugar field labour within the context of the history of the

2 *Australian Sugar Journal*, 15 December 1948, p.515; Burrows & Morton, *The Canecutters*, p.121.

3 "Without these immigrants, the record crops of 1948 and 1949 could not have been harvested."*Aust. Sugar Journal*, 15 Feb 1950, p.687.

world's cane sugar industries' labour problems and solutions is of particular historical interest.

Of all the unskilled labouring jobs the displaced persons were directed to, canecutting in North Queensland was undoubtedly that most foreign to their former experiences. Once in the sugar towns they entered another world. Adjustments had to be made to a tropical climate, small town life and culture, and the loneliness and primitive living conditions of distant farms. Skills of a back-breaking labour had to be learnt; the body's initial 'breaking-in' period had to be endured. These 'New Australians', 'reffo's', 'Balts' were of curiosity value in small towns where men of their nationalities had never before been encountered and certainly some met with prejudice and ill-feeling. As canecutters, they assumed a singular identity fraught with popular misconceptions of which they were largely unaware. They no more conformed to the popular images of the canecutter than did their Australian co-workers.

Canecutting, its skills and daily routine; the life in work and leisure; the mateship; the relationships; the itinerant nature of the occupation; the importance of the canecutters to the sugar communities, within the Australian context has long awaited detailed study. A curious lifestyle that both broke and made men, demanding such prodigious physical effort it was felt that a man had to be akin to a beast of burden or a superhuman hero to persevere, it gave rise to surprising amount of varied and colourful literary work.

The number of canecutters required by the sugar industry grew rapidly after the Second World War, intensifying the drive to perfect mechanical harvesters. At the height of the 1951 season 6134 cutters were employed in Queensland: in 1955, 8754.[4] Within twenty years manual cutting had been superseded completely. In 1973 there was no call-up for canecutters in the Cairns area:[5] in December 1977 all reference to manual canecutters was deleted from the Sugar Industry Award.[6]

The displaced persons employed as canecutters, made an invaluable contribution to the industry, particularly between 1949 and 1951 when there was no alternative to manual cutting. The life of the canecutter was one of back-breaking toil, yet it was tinged with colour and romance.[7] Its passing was viewed with nostalgia by all whom it touched. With their different backgrounds, languages, attitudes and practices displaced persons brought an exotic new colour to that life just as it was destined to pass away for ever.

4 A.S.P.A. *Annual Report*, 1956, p.7.

5 Bolton, "Memories before the 18th Doll", p.2.

6 "Canecutters' Era at End", *Courier-Mail*, 15 December 1979, p.15. See also F. Johnston, "Canecutters' Award whittled down to a one-man stand", *Australian*, 21 December 1977, p.3.

7 Gollschewsky, "The Yesterdays and Todays of the Sugarcane Industry", p.76.

APPENDIX A

TABLES DETAILING NUMBERS OF DISPLACED PERSONS RESETTLED IN AUSTRALIA UNDER THE I.R.O. SCHEME

TABLE 1: REFUGEES RESETTLED BY THE I.R.O. IN COUNTRIES OUTSIDE EUROPE EXCLUDING ISRAEL), BY NATIONALITY AND COUNTRY OF DESTINATION. 1947-51

(in thousands)

Nationality	Canada	U.S.A.	Venezuela	Brazil	Argentina	Australia	Misc.	Total
Balts	21.3	77.5	1.7	1.4	1.4	35.7	2.0	141.1
Hungarians	7.5	16.7	2.0	3.1	3.1	13.3	2.2	47.9
Poles	47.0	110.6	2.8	7.8	6.6	60.3	5.7	240.8
Russians and Ukrainians	23.2	60.7	2.7	6.4	4.4	25.2	5.6	128.2
Czechoslovaks	5.0	8.1	0.8	1.5	0.6	9.9	1.4	28.2
Yugoslavs	9.8	17.2	2.0	2.6	10.1	23.4	3.8	68.9
Miscellaneous and not stated	8.8	38.1	5.2	6.1	6.5	14.4	12.0	91.1
Total	123.5	238.9	17.3	28.8	32.7	182.1	33.0	746.2

Source: International Labour Office, *International Migration 1945-1957*. p.181.

APPENDIX A (contd)

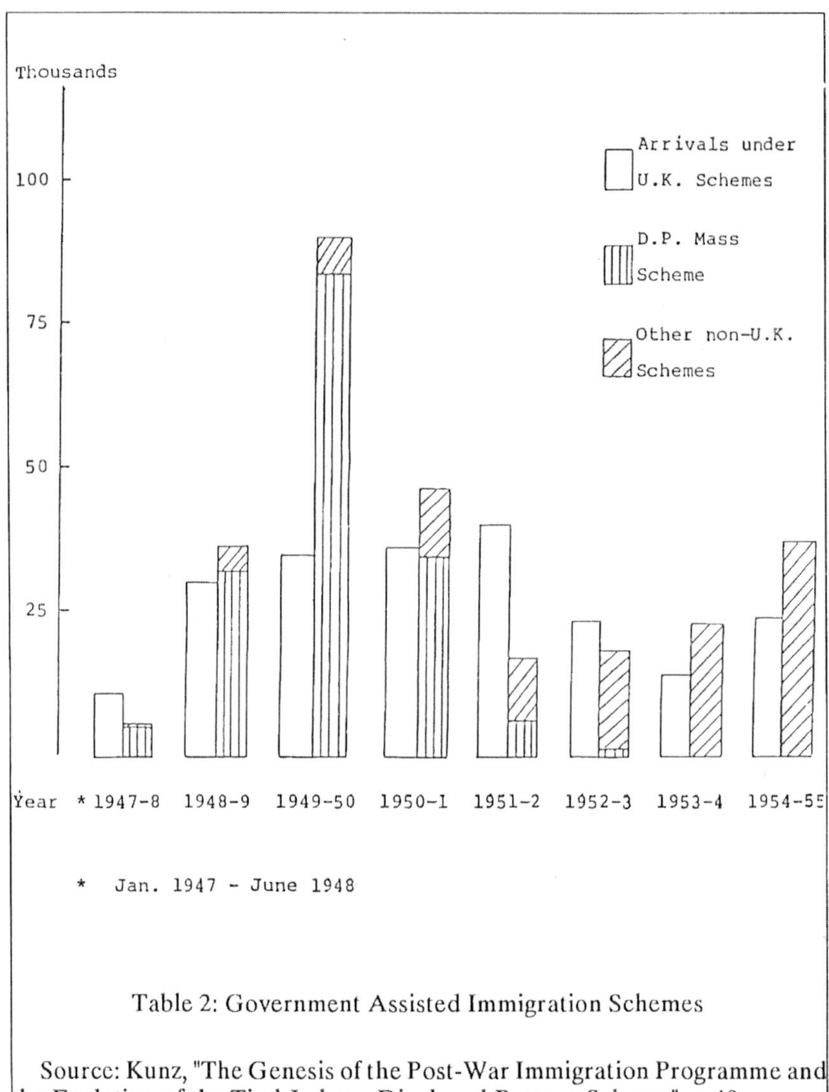

Table 2: Government Assisted Immigration Schemes

Source: Kunz, "The Genesis of the Post-War Immigration Programme and the Evolution of the Tied-Labour Displaced Persons Scheme", p.40.

APPENDIX B

I.R.O. LIVING CENTER
FREE LIVING REFUGEES
ELIGIBILITY SCREENING
TRADE TESTING
COUNSELLING AND ORIENTATION
VOCATIONAL TRAINING
LANGUAGE TRAINING
PRESELECTION
INITIAL DOCUMENTATION
MEDICAL REHABILITATION
INITIAL MEDICAL EXAMINATION
I.R.O. RESETTLEMENT CENTER
GOVERNMENT SELECTION MISSIONS
MED EXAM FOR FITNESS FOR TRAVEL
CUSTOMS CHECK
BAGGAGE CHECK
MOVEMENT DOCUMENTATION
CONSULAR INTERVIEW
MEDICAL TEST
SECURITY INTERVIEW
LITERACY TEST
LABOR SELECTOR
SPECIAL TRADE TESTING
HOSPITAL
SECURITY DOCUMENTATION
I.R.O. STAGING CENTER
ORIENTATION AND LANGUAGE COURSES
MOVEMENT DOCUMENTATION
MED EXAM FOR FITNESS FOR TRAVEL
I.R.O. EMBARKATION CENTER
FINAL MEDICAL CHECK
FINAL SECURITY CHECK
PORT OF EMBARKATION
I.R.O. IDENTIFICATION CHECK

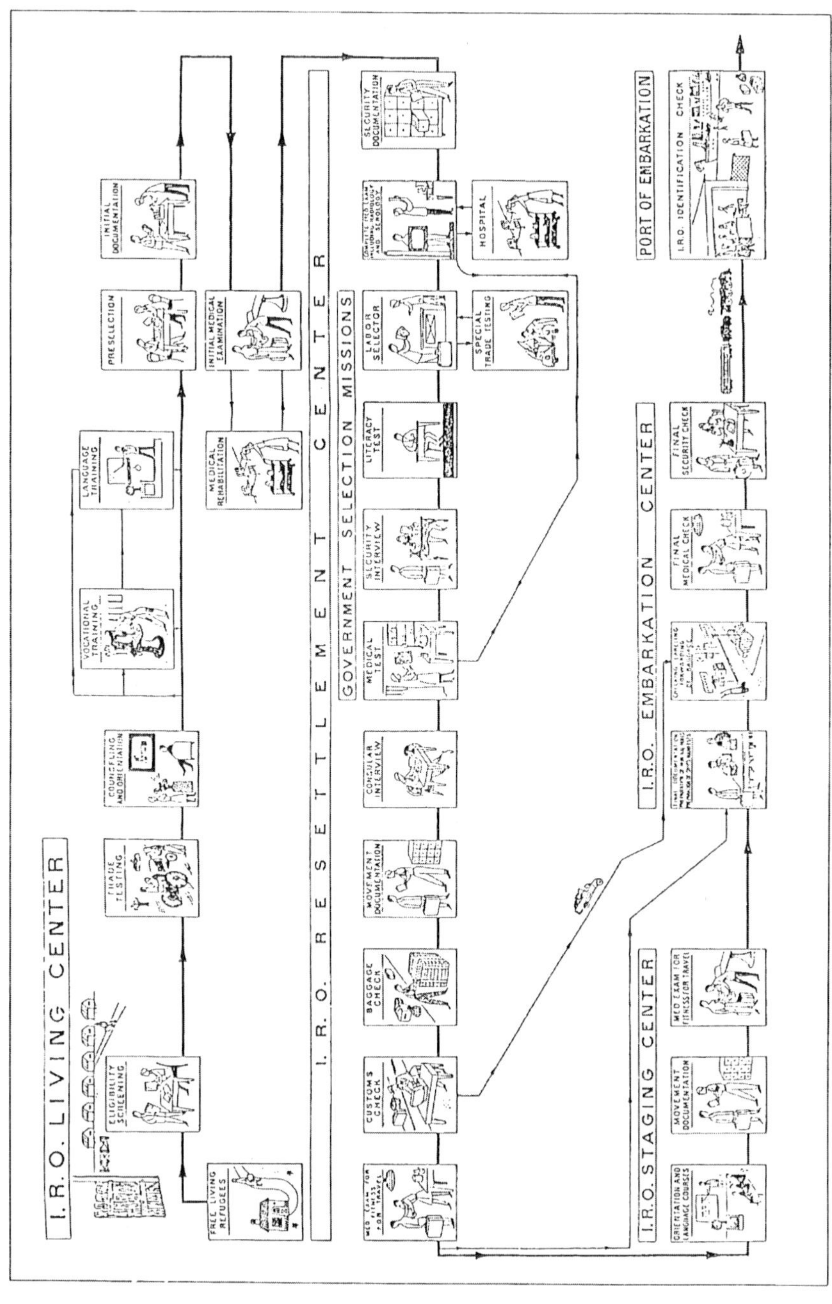

APPENDIX C:

FORM OF UNDERTAKING

(COPY)

Undertaking signed by emigrants who left Germany:

Undertaking

I hereby certify that the above particulars are true in every respect, that I have made myself familiar with the conditions under which displaced persons can emigrant to Australia. I fully understand that I must remain in the employment found for me for at least one year and that I shall not be permitted to change that employment during that period without the consent of the Department of Immigration.

Certified Correct Copy.
Commonwealth Employment Service.
BONEGILLA. VIC.

'AA:CRS A434, 1939-1950; 50/3/13 Pt 2'.

APPENDIX D: CERTIFICATE OF EXEMPTION

(COPY)

COMMONWEALTH OF AUSTRALIA

Immigration Act 1901-1940

Number ____________________

Form No. 2.

State of ______________________________ Port of __________________

Date of Issue __________________ 19 _________

CERTIFICATE OF EXEMPTION

THIS IS TO CERTIFY THAT ___________________________________

who is described hereunder, is authorised to enter or remain in the Commonwealth without being subject to any provisions of the Immigration Act 1901-1940 restricting entry into or stay in the Commonwealth.

This certificate shall be in force for a period of

months from the ____________________ day of _____________ 19 ____

Nationality _____________ Birthplace __________________ Age _____

Particular Marks ____

Occupation ____

Signature of Person exempted __________________________________

____

Commonwealth Migration Officer

Melbourne

____

(By authority of the Minister for Immigration)

AA:CRS MP243/3, 1943-1950; 1-41.

APPENDIX E:

A MEDICAL REPORT FORM USED IN AUSTRALIA AT RECEPTION AND TRAINING CENTRES
(COPY)

MEDICAL REPORT FORM AND PHYSICAL RESTRICTIONS ANALYSIS

Incapable of														Vision corrected			Hearing			Is patient incapable of working under these conditions?									
1	2	3	4	5	6	7	8	9	10	11	12	13	14	15	16	17	18	19	20	21	22	23	24	25	26	27	28	29	30
100% standing	100% walking	Much walking	Any kneeling	Any stooping	Any climbing	Much pulling	Much pushing	Nimble use of fingers	Use of both hands	Use of right hand	Use of left hand	Lifting from 10-25 lbs.	Lifting over 25 lbs.	Good (20/40 8 14/28)	Fair (20/60 8 14/42)	Poor	Good (20/10)	Fair (20/5)	Poor	Hot	Cold	Wet	Humid	Slipping or tripping conditions	Dusty	Fumes	Noisy	Heights	Any skin irritants

DIAGNOSIS: ....

COMMENTS: ....

....

....

NAME.. R. & T.C.. Examining Physician..

Number

Source: 'AA: CRS A445, 1951-1955; 179/9/5 Pt3'.

APPENDIX F:

LETTER SENT TO IMMIGRANTS IN RECEPTION AND TRAINING CENTRE ADVISING HIM OF WORK PLACEMENT

(COPY)

COMMONWEALTH OF AUSTRALIA

COMMONWEALTH EMPLOYMENT SERVICE

Telephone:
Branxton 31.

Reception & Training Centre
GRETA No. 2.

In any correspondence
please quote:
L. No. 1036/Q50

Dear Sir

I desire to advise that, as discussed, arrangements have been made to place you in the employ of CANE GROWERS ASSOCIATION/Qld. at MULGRAVE/Qld as cane cutter.

You should commence work on arrival.

The hours and/or shifts will be 40 hours per 5 days.

Your wages will be award rates.

While they remain at that level, deductions from your wages are likely to be approximately

Tax Deductions

such deductions totalling

leaving a net pay of about

You will leave GRETA 2 on Monday 4/9/50 at 11am. and the travel arrangements made for you are as follows:

Depart Greta 2	12.55 pm.	4/9/50
Arrive Taree	5.51 pm.	4/9/50
Depart Taree	6.51 pm.	4/9/50
Arrive Brisbane	8.15 am.	5/9/50;
met by DEO		
Depart Brisbane	2.40 pm.	5/9/50
Arrive CAIRNS	11 am.	
7/9/50; met by Employer.		

The address of the District Employment Officer of the Commonwealth Employment Service whom you should consult if you wish to make any enquiries about your wages, or working conditions, or if you need advice or information on any other matter, is Spencer St., CAIRNS and his telephone number is CAIRNS 2817. He will be glad to help you, and there is no charge for this service.

You will remember that the Certificate of Exemption granted to you under the Immigration Act 1901-1940, requires you, for a period of up to two years, to engage in such employment as the Commonwealth Employment Service on behalf of the Minister for Immigration approves. A change of employment can only be arranged if there are very special reasons to justify it.

YOU MUST NOT LEAVE THE EMPLOYMENT MENTIONED ABOVE UNLESS YOU HAVE FIRST APPLIED TO THE DISTRICT EMPLOYMENT OFFICER AND RECEIVED HIS APPROVAL TO DO SO.

Yours faithfully

(signed)
J.A. KRAUSE
Officer in Charge, Employment
Service, GRETA 2.

Meal money : 1/2/6.

Form E.S. S S L & N.S. Revised 6/49.

Original in possession of Yugoslav canecutter DN, interviewed 28 May 1983.

APPENDIX G: CERTIFICATE OF AUTHORITY TO REMAIN IN AUSTRALIA

(COPY)

COMMONWEALTH OF AUSTRALIA

CERTIFICATE OF AUTHORITY TO REMAIN

IN AUSTRALIA

THIS IS TO CERTIFY that approval has been given for the removal of the limitation imposed under the Immigration Act upon the stay in Australia of

who is the holder of Aliens Registration Certificate No.

is now entitled to remain here indefinitely subject to the laws of the Commonwealth governing residence in Australia.

This Certificate will be sufficient evidence that is no longer regarded as a temporary resident of the Commonwealth.

Dated this day of 19

By authority of the
Minister for Immigration

This document is not a Certificate of Naturalisation and does not confer Australian citizenship or British nationality.

Information relating to the future obligation under the Aliens Act, 1947 of the grantee of this Certificate and details of the procedure for the acquisition of Australian citizenship and British nationality appear on the reverse side of this document.

Should the grantee of this Certificate desire to leave Asutralia temporarily before becoming an Australian citizen, return here would be facilitated by obtaining a Re-Entry Permit before leaving.

Original in possession of Yugoslaw canecutter K.B., questionnaire completed early 1982.

APPENDIX H:

It is not claimed that the experiences of those interviewed were necessarily representative of all displaced person canecutters. The inspiration for this book was the author's father; interviewing started with him and those with whom he cut cane. The gangs formed at Bonegilla and Greta tended to be homogenous in nationality; consequently most of those interviewed early were of my father's nationality: Yugoslav. A conscious attempt was then made to contact former canecutters of other nationalities. This was not easy. Many had left the district years before and could not be traced. Many had died; a few had become drifters, unmarried and alcohol dependent.

Of those contacted not more than half-a-dozen declined to be interviewed. But some of those interviewed were a little uneasy over the lengthy probing of their memories and firm promises of anonymity had to be given.

From experience it was found most satisfactory to record interviews by hand-written notes; only three of the twenty-two interviews undertaken were taped. Quotations from notes cannot be as strictly verbatim as those from tapes; though confident of having captured accurately not merely the sense but the idiom, I have substituted the third for the first person in all such quotations.

All tapes, notes made during interviews and completed questionnaires remain in the author's possession.

TABLE 1: SUPPLEMENTARY PARTICULARS OF THE DISPLACED PERSON CANECUTTER INTERVIEWEES

INITIALS	NATIONALITY	YEAR OF ARRIVAL	SHIP	AGE ON ARRIVAL	FAMILY BACKGROUND	MARITAL STATUS ON ARRIVAL	RECEPTION AND TRAINING CENTRE	PREVIOUS OCCUPATION/ TRADE	PRESENT OCCUPATION	WIFE'S NATIONALITY	METHOD OF RECORDING	INTERVIEW DATE
A.P.	Yugoslav	1950	Skaubryn	18	Farming	Single	Bonegilla	Fitter and Turner	Farmer	Australian (Italian parentage)	Hand	5/3/1983
A.S.	Polish	1948	Strathnaver	31	Landscaping business	Single	Bathurst Army Camp	Teacher/Army Officer	Worker at Sugar Terminal till retirement	Australian	Tape	8/11/1984
B.I.	Russian	1950	Dundalk Bay	34	Mixed farming Parents had died.	Married	Greta 2	Storeman. Learnt trade in Germany. Shoemaker	Yardman till retirement	German	Tape	7/11/1984
D.N.	Yugoslav	1950	Goya	25	Large farm owners	Single	Greta 2	Technical College student: engineering	Gardener at shopping centre	Australian	Hand	28/5/1983
F.N.	Ukrainian	1949	Mohammedi	32	Farming	Married	Bonegilla	Labourer	Cane farmer	Ukrainian	Tape	3/11/1984
G.M.	Yugoslav	1951	Skaubryn	22	Farming.Family had migrated with him.	Single	Bonegilla	Labourer	Taxi Owner/ Driver	Australian	Questionnaire	Completed Nov. 1984
G.Z.	Lithuanian	1948	General Black	24	Store and small farm	Single	Bonegilla	Tailor	Farm labourer till retirement	Australian (Basque parentage)	Hand	30/10/1984
I.D.	Yugoslav	1949	Mohammedi	40	Labouring	Married	Bonegilla	Labourer	Labourer till retirement	Austrian	Hand	5/11/1984
J.P.	Yugoslav	1950	Mohammedi	35	Industrial worker-father (had migrated to USA and later returned home)	Married	Greta 2	Industrial worker then Policeman	School Groundsman till retirement	Yugoslav	Hand	31/3/1984
K.B.	Yugoslav	1949	Mohammedi	22	Tradesman-father	Single	Bonegilla	Surveyor	Brewery: Person-nel & Industrial Relations Officer	Australian	Questionnaire	
K.M.	Polish	1949	Goya	29	Labouring	Married	Greta 2	Farm Labourer	Labourer till retirement	German	Hand	9/11/1984
M.L.	Yugoslav	1949	Mohammedi	24	Farming	Single	Bonegilla	Commenced Butcher trade	Brewery worker	Italian nationality Yugoslav born	Hand	15/5/1983
M.M.	Yugoslav	1948	General Black	23	Small shop	Single	Bonegilla	University student Engineering	Cane farmer	Australian (Italian parentage	Hand	21/10/1984
R.C.	Czech	1951	Skaubryn	21	Tobacconist business	Single	Bonegilla	Boilermaker	Boilermaker at Sugar Mill	Australian	Hand	8/3/1985
T.A.	Yugoslav	1948	Protea	28	Farming Parents had died	Single	Bonegilla	3 months off Chef Diploma	Labourer till retirement	Australian (Italian parentage	Hand	14/5/1983
V.V.	Yugoslav	1949	Mohammedi	20	Glassmaker - father	Single	Bonegilla	Fitter and Turner	Labourer till retirement	Australian	Questionnaire & discussions	Completed 1983

TABLE 2: OTHER INTERVIEWEES

INITIALS	NATIONALITY	RELEVANT DETAILS	METHOD OF RECORDING	INTERVIEW DATE
A.A.	Yugoslav	Post World War I migrant. Farmer - employed displaced persons gangs.	Hand	6/3/1983
I.U.	Yugoslav	Refugee brought to Australia under the I.C.E.M. Scheme - 1954.	Hand	29/5/1983
K.C.	Australian	Former A.W.U. Organizer	Hand	1/4/1984
M.G.	Yugoslav	Post World War I migrant. Farmer - employed and befriended displaced persons gangs.	Hand	6/3/1983
N.B.	Yugoslav	Migrated as a young teenager Pre World War II. Worked with and befriended displaced persons.	Hand	10/11/1984
S.B.	Australian	Farmer - employed displaced persons gangs. Formerly Chairman and Committee Member of Mill Suppliers'Committee.	Hand	31/10/1984
T.Z.	Yugoslav	Refugee who migrated to Australia as a nominated immigrant - 1955.	Hand	3/1/1983

APPENDIX I: CANE KNIFE ADVERTISEMENTS

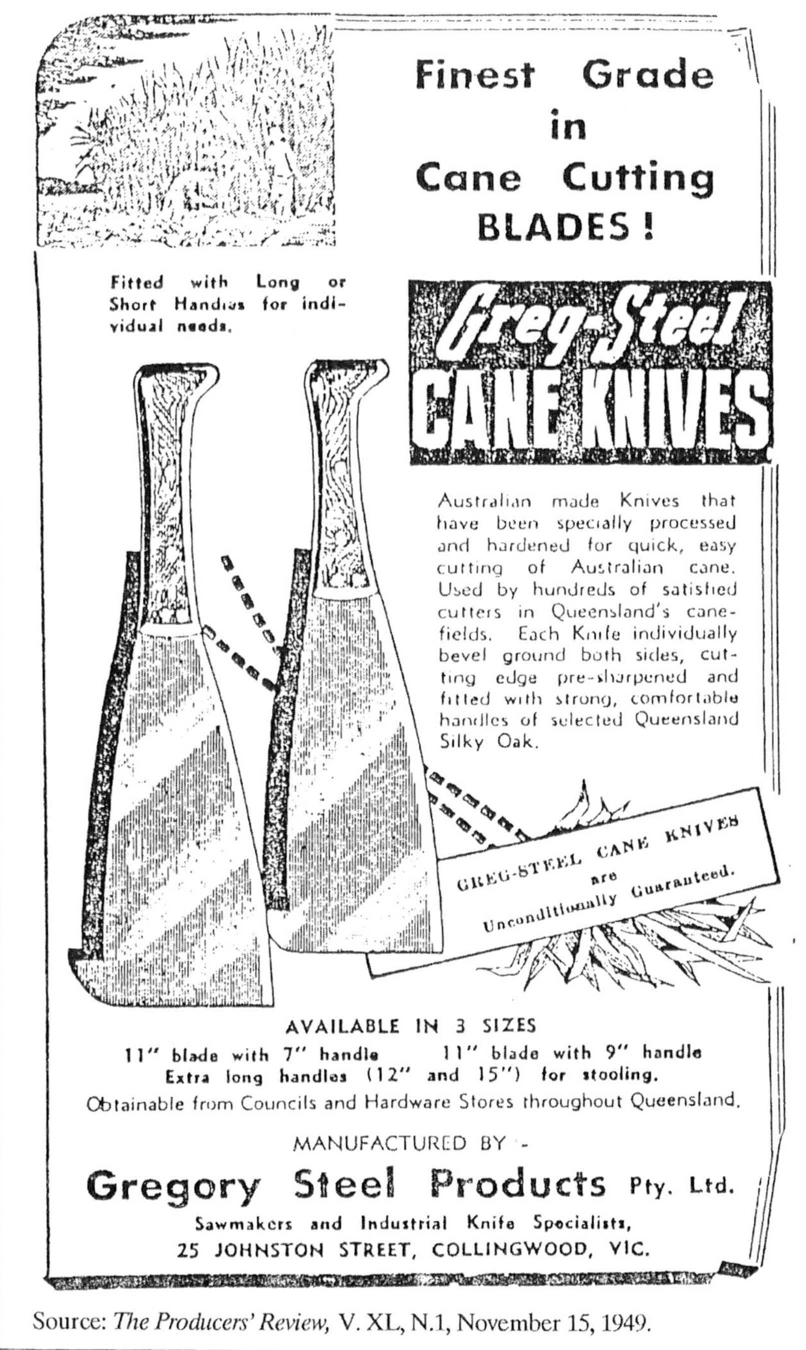

Source: *The Producers' Review,* V. XL, N.1, November 15, 1949.

APPENDIX I (contd):

"QUEENSLAND ACE." Here is a range of Cane Knives of proved excellence. Made from the finest Sheffield steel they keep their edge and do not need a lot of re-sharpening. A range of patterns and handles is available. Ask for "Queensland Ace" Cane Knives on your next order.

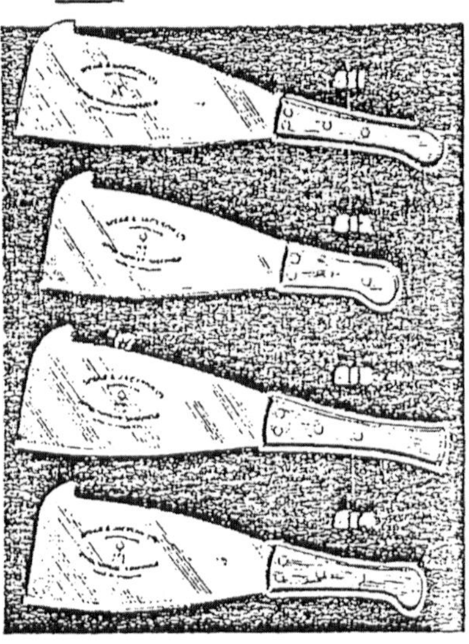

511 Length 20in., bright blade, 11½in. x 18 gauge, handle 8½in., weight approx. 12½lb. dozen.

512 Length 17¼in., bright blade, 11¼in. x 18 gauge, handle 6in., weight approx. 11½lb. dozen.

513 Length 20in., bright blade, 11¼in. x 18 gauge, handle 8¾in., weight approx. 13lb. dozen.

514 Length 18½in., bright blade, 11in., x 18 gauge, handle 7½in., weight approx. 12¾lb. dozen.

'QUEENSLAND ACE'
Hard and Sharp
CANE KNIVES

Factory Representatives:—
THOMAS C. BROWN & COMPANY PTY. LTD.
BROUGHTON HOUSE, 181 CLARENCE ST., SYDNEY, N.S.W.
Telegrams & Cables: "TECBROWN," SYDNEY. Telephone MA9174. BOX 1634, G.P.O.
Distribution is made only through wholesale channels.

MANUFACTURED BY SPEAR & JACKSON LTD. SHEFFIELD ENGLAND

CZ.3

Trade with our Advertisers, and always mention "The Producers' Review."

Source: *The Producers' Review*, V. XL. N.1, November 15, 1949.

APPENDIX J:

INTERVIEW GUIDE

Originally prepared as a guide for use in personal interviews, this questionnaire was also sent to respondents whom it was impracticable to interview on account of distance. They were asked to answer each question as fully as possible in writing.

Place of Birth: Country
Region
Town/Village
Farming/Industrial/Fishing
Father's occupation/trade
Marital status at time of migration
now
Current residence i.e.:
this address
this area
town
other (give details)
Number of children
How many years of education did you have?
Are you qualified for any trade or profession?
If so, what?

Was there a history of migration from your area?
If so, where to?
What were your main reasons for emigrating?
Why did you migrate to Australia?
Some migrants have described their migration as "It was like going for a drive on Sunday, you didn't really mind where". Was it like that for you?
Did you know of any people in Australia?
If so, where had they settled?
What work were they engaged in?
Was there any specific area you wanted to migrate to in Australia
If so, where and why?
Have you sponsored any one to come to Australia?
If yes, relationship to you: relative/friend/other
Do you have any relatives living in Australia?
If yes, relationship to you: relative/friend/other
Where do they live in Australia?

Date of leaving your homeland

Date of leaving Europe

Age at migration

What was your last job before coming to Australia?

Where did you go to, from your homeland/after the war (e.g.: Italy; Austria; Germany; to a displaced persons' camp)

If to a camp, what was life like in this camp?

(a) food
(b) living quarters
(c) company
(d) entertainment
(e) morale

Were you divided into national groups?

If not, did you keep company only with your own countrymen?

What national groups were there?

What was the screening process for migration? (e.g.: medicals; ques tions asked)

Were you aware of the two year labour contract at this stage?

From which European port did you leave?

Name of ship?

What were your feelings as the boat finally pulled away from the dock?

Did you intend to return, or was it a permanent departure?

What was the journey like?

(a) food
(b) company
(c) entertainment
(d) morale
(e) changes of climate
(f) language classes

How did you feel at the first sight of the Australian shoreline?

Date of arrival in Australia

What happened from disembarkation to arrival in a migrants' camp?

Name of migrants' camp.

How long did you stay in the migrants' camp?

What was life like in the migrants' camp?

(a) food
(b) company
(c) entertainment
(d) morale
(e) effects of climate
(f) language classes

Were you divided into national groups in the camp?

How soon were you allocated a job?

Where were you to work?

What was the job?
How did you feel about having to do this type of work?
How did you travel to this job?
Was there a group of you?
Were there any other countrymen in this group?
How did the change in climate and scenery affect you?
Who met you on arrival at your destination?
What happened from your arrival to the evening before you were able to commence work?
What were your impressions of Australians up to this point?
Were you writing home to relatives at this stage?
If not, why not?
Jobs held in Australia prior to canecutting: Year/Job/Place

Date you commenced canecutting
Where was the farm (i.e.: nearest town)
What nationality was the first farmer you worked for?
What was the national composition of the first gang you worked with?
How many of them were experienced canecutters?
What were your reactions to the living quarters (barracks)?
What was the first day of canecutting like?
How long did it take for you to feel you were carrying your weight in the gang?
In this first season were you affected by the:
(a) climate
(b) food
(c) work
What friends did you make?
Did you socialize with?
(a) only countrymen
(b) also Australians
(c) only Australians
(d) various nationalities
What did you do in your spare time?
Did you become friendly with any Australian girls in this first season?
What problems did you have, as a migrant, in becoming friendly with Australian girls?
Were there any girls from your homeland you could have/did become friendly with?
What did you do in the first 'slack'?
Did you go back to canecutting the next season or any other season?
Year/farmer/area/number of countrymen in the gang/job in the slack
Did you break your contract?

If so, what were the repercussions?
Once you fulfilled your two year contract did you find a job in your trade/profession?
If so, where?
If not, why not?
If you kept canecutting, was it money that attracted you back?
If not, what did?
Did you save your money?
Was saving money for a piece of land and/or a house of most importance from your first days in Australia?
If so, why?
Were you sending money home?
If so, when did you stop sending money home?
Did you ever have difficulties making friends or finding a job because you were a migrant?
If so, what were the occasions when you had difficulties and why?
What nationality is/was your wife?
If she is Australian, did it take you long to be accepted by her family?
Were you still canecutting when you married?
If so, did being married change your relationship with the gang?
Did you continue to live in barracks?
Did buying a home of your own become more important once you were married?
Were you ever a ganger?
If so, what did the job entail?
Did you leave canecutting before the mechanical cane harvester began to be used on most farms?
If so, why?
If not, why did you eventually leave canecutting?
For what job did you leave canecutting?
Year of last 'cut/
How did you feel when your canecutting days came to an end?
What jobs have you held since leaving canecutting?
Year/job/place (up to and including present job)
Have you ever been unemployed in Australia?
If yes, what was the longest period of unemployment?
When and how did you become a member of the A.W.U.?
Do you now have any health problems you would attribute to your days of canecutting?
Describe the canecutting job.

Nationality
Date of naturalization
Why did you decide to become a naturalized Australian?

If not, why not?

Have you been back to your homeland?

If so, when?

Have you ever thought of returning to live in your homeland?

If so, why?

If not, why not?

Were you ever/or are you a member of a nationals' club here in Australia?

Did/do you belong to any other clubs? Name of club(s)?

If yes, how often did/do you go there?

Are there any other places you met/meet for a talk with other countrymen?

Do you now have mostly friends who are your countrymen
some friends who are your countrymen
no friends who are your countrymen

QUESTIONS ASKED OF YUGOSLAVS ONLY:

Here in Australia, have you ever been friendly with Yugoslavs from different regions of Yugoslavia?

Did you ever witness quarrels, here in Australia, between Yugoslavs from different regions? (e.g.: Serbs/Croats)

If so, what form did these quarrels take?

Yugoslavs, here in Australia, seem to have gained a reputation of being a knife-wielding, fiery lot. How do you think they gained this reputation?

Do you speak your native tongue in the home?

If not, why not?

What do you regard as the greatest single difficulty or problem that you have had to face in trying to settle down in Australia?

Since living in Australia have you achieved as much in life as you expected to?

Do you ever regret your decision to migrate to Australia? (e.g.: your work, your housing, your friends, your lifestyle)

BIBLIOGRAPHY

PRIMARY SOURCES

OFFICIAL, MANUSCRIPT
AUSTRALIAN ARCHIVES

Attorney-General's Dept:

CRSA432 Correspondence files, multiple number series, 1939-1947

47/287 Refugee & Displaced Persons - Immigration to Australia - Government Policy, 1947

Dept. of Immigration:

CRSA434 Correspondence files, Class 3 (Non-British) European migrants, 1939-1950

50/3/13 Displaced Persons Employment Policy, 1950 Pt 2

50/3/1788 Press cuttings encourage migration - other than from UK, 1947-1948

CRSA436 Correspondence files, Class 5 (British Migrants) 1945-1950

50/5/3482 Decentralisation and Rural Development - Suggested Disembarkation of Some Migrants at North Queensland Ports, 1951

CRSA445 Correspondence files, multiple number series (Policy Matters), 1947

140/4/5 Commonwealth Immigration Advisory Council - Agenda & Minutes of 5th Meeting, 1947

140/4/9 Commonwealth Immigration Advisory Council - Agenda & Minutes of 9th Meeting, 1949

140/4/12 Commonwealth Immigration Advisory Council -Agenda & Minutes of 12th Meeting, 1950

140/4/14 Commonwealth Immigration Advisory Council - Agenda & Minutes of 14th Meeting, 1951

140/4/15 Commonwealth Immigration Advisory Council -Agenda & Minutes of 15th Meeting, 1951

142/4/1 Committee on Rural Production. Commonealth Immigration Planning Council, Pt 1

145/3/4 Conference of Commonwealth & State Ministers on Immigration, 1948. Pt 1

145/3/5 Conference of Commonwealth & State Ministers on Immigration, 1948, Pt 2

145/3/7 Conference of Commonwealth & State Ministers on Immigration, 1949, Pt 2

162/3/4 Manpower & Immigration - Northern Australia, 1951-1955
179/1/3 Queensland Sugar Industry - Employment of Migrants, 1947-1951, Pts 1,2,3
179/1/4 Queensland Sugar Industry - Employment of Migrants, 1951-1954, Pt 4
179/1/6 Introduction of Skilled Tradesmen from Europe for Building Industry, 1951-1955
179/9/3 Displaced Persons - Employment Opportunities Policy, 1951-1955, Pt 1
179/9/5 Displaced Persons - Employment Opportunities Policy, 1951-1955, Pt 3

CRS BT60/1 Correspondence files, 1946-1948
Q48/5437 Balts for Employment in Sugar Industry in Queensland & New South Wales, 1946-1948

Prime Minister's Department

CRS A461 Correspondence files, multiple number series, 1934-1950; Y349/3/5 Migration - Europe. Refugees, 1938-1948

Dept. of External Affairs (II)

CRSA1838 Correspondence files, multiple number series, 1948-
861/5/2 I.R.O. Australian Delegation Reports, 1948

Dept. of Labour & National Service

CRSMT157/8 Employment Division files, 1947-1948
ZV2010 Displaced Persons Policy, Nov 1947 - June 1948

CRSMP243/3 Circulars, Directorate of Manpower & Commonwealth Employment Service, 1943-1950; 1-41
Box 26.Commonwealth Employment Service - Immigration Circulars, 1946/1950

CRSMP574/1 General correspondence of the Secretariat and Administrative & Industrial Relations Divisions, 1940-1950; 573/2/23 Displaced Persons, 1940-1950, Pt 1

OFFICIAL PUBLICATIONS: COMMONWEALTH OF AUSTRALIA

Official Statistics
Demography, No.64 (1946) to No.70 (1955-58)

Official Year Book
No.37 (1946-7) to No.42 (1956)

Parliamentary Papers
1946-53

Senate and House of Representatives, Debates

1946-51

Immigration Policies and Australia's Population: a Green Paper
Australian Population & Immigration Council, Canberra, 1977
Immigration, Policy and Progress
A.A. Calwell, Canberra, 1949
Cultural Background Papers: Yugoslavia
Dept. of Education & Youth Affairs, Canberra, 1983

OFFICIAL PUBLICATIONS: QUEENSLAND

Queensland Government Gazette
CLXX (1948) - CLXXVIII (1951)
Queensland Industrial Gazette
Sept. 1947 - June 1950
Legislative Assembly, Debates
CXCII (1947) - 201 (1952)
Legislative Assembly, Parliamentary Papers
1947-1952

INTERVIEWS, QUESTIONNAIRES, ETC

(i) Displaced Person Interviewed - hand recorded:

AP 5 March 1983
DN 28 May 1983
GZ 30 Oct 1984
ID 5 Nov 1984
JP 31 March 1984
KM 9 Nov 1984
ML 15 May 1983
MM 21 Oct 1984
RC 8 March 1985
TA 14 May 1983

(ii) Displaced Person Interviewees - taped interviews:

AS 8 Nov 1984
BI 7 Nov 1984
FN 3 Nov 1984

(iii) Displaced Persons - questionnaires completed:

GM 1984
KB 1982
VV 1983 (Also written communication 1982;

discussions 1984)

AA 6 March 1983
KC 31 Oct 1984
IU 29 May 1983
MG 1 April 1984
NB 10 Nov 1984
TZ 3 Jan 1983

Other Informants - informal discussions:

SB 1984

MISCELLANEOUS

Commonwealth Government of Australia. *Certificate of Authority to Remain in Australia.* (Original belonging to KB.)

Commonwealth Government of Australia. *Letter sent to Immigrant in Reception and Training Centre advising him of Work Placement.* (Original belonging to DN.)

Private Photographic Collections. BI, DN, FN, GZ, ML, RC, VV

SECONDARY SOURCES

BOOKS, PAMPHLETS, ETC

Adamson, A.H., *Sugar Without Slaves: The Political Economy of British Guiana 1838-1904*, Yale U.P., New Haven, 1972

Association of Agriculture., *A Sugar Cane Farm in North Queensland: Farm Study Scheme*, The Association, London, 1963

Baume, F.E., *Burnt Sugar*, Macquarie Head Press, Sydney, 1934

Bell, A., *The Story of the Sugar Industry in Queensland*, Q.U.P., Brisbane, 1956

Birrell, R. & Hay, C. , *The Immigration Issue in Australia: A Sociological Symposium*. Department of Sociology, La Trobe University, Victoria, 1978

Borin, V.L., *The Uprooted Survive: a Tale of Two Continents*, Allen & Unwin, London, 1959

Borrie, W.D., "Australia's New Population Pattern" in Holt, H.E. (et.al.) *Australia and the Migrant*, Angus and Robertson, Sydney, 1953

Borrie, W.D, . "Australia" in Thomas, B. (ed.) *Economics of International Migration*. Macmillan, London, 1958

Borrie, W.D. & Jupp, K., *The Economic Demography of Immigration to Australia*. World Population Conference Papers 2, U.N., N.Y., 1954/1955

Bosi, P., *Farewell Australia*, Kurunda Publications, Sydney, 1972

Bouscaren, A.T., *International Migrations since 1945*. Frederick A. Praeger, N.Y., 1963

Burrows, G. & Morton, C. , *The Canecutters*, Melbourne U.P., 1986

Calwell, A.A., "The Why and How of Post-War Migration" in Holt, H.E. (et.al.). *Australia and the Migrant*. Angus and Robertson, Sydney, 1953

Cell, J.W., "The New Australians" in Preston, K. (ed.). *Contemporary Australia: Studies in History, Politics and Economics*, Duke U.P., Durham, North Carolina, 1969

Courtenay, P.P., *Plantation Agriculture*, G. Bell and Sons, London, 1965

Courtenay, P.P. (et.al.). , *The Settlement and Population Characteristics, Johnstone District, Queensland Sugar Coast*, Monograph Series, Occasional Paper No.1. Department of Geography, J.C.U., 1974

Craton, M. & Walvin, J., *A Jamaican Plantation: The History of Worthy Park 1670-1970*, W.H. Allen, London, 1970

Curlewis, F.C.P., *An Aspect of the Australian Sugar Industry: The Co-ordination of State Control and Internal Organization*, A Paper read before the Queensland Branch of the Economic Society of Australia and New Zealand. 12 May 1933

De Bres, J., Campbell, R. & Harris, P., *Migrant Labour in the Pacific*, N.Z. Resource Centre for World Development, Corso, 1974

Devanny, J., *Sugar Heaven*, Modern Publishers, Sydney, 1936

Devanny, J., *By Tropic Sea and Jungle*, Angus and Robertson, Sydney, 1944

Donaldson, R., Joseph, M., & Braddon, R., *Cane!* Sphere Books, London, 1967

Easterby, H.T., *The Queensland Sugar Industry: An Historical Review*, Bureau of Sugar Experiment Stations in Queensland

Eisenberg, P.L., *The Sugar Industry in Pernambuco: Modernization without Change 1840-1910*, California U.P., Berkeley, 1974

Eisner, G., *Jamaica, 1830-1930: A Study in Economic Growth*, Manchester U.Press, 1961

Frings, J.P., *The Australian Cane Sugar Industry: From Virgin Soil to Consumer*, A.S.P.A. Limited, Brisbane

Gillion, K.L., *The Fiji Indians: Challenge to European Dominance 1920-1946*, A.N.U., Canberra, 1977

Grenfell Price, A., *The White Man in the Tropics and the Problem of North Australia*, Radio Broadcast, 11th and 18th July 1934

Grenfell Price, A., *White Settlers in the Tropics*, American Geographical Society, New York, 1939

Hempel, J.A., *Italians in Queensland: Some Aspects of the Post-War Settlement of Italian Immigrants*, A.N.U., Canberra, 1959

Holborn, L.W., *The International Refugee Organization: A Specialized Agency of the U.N. Its History and Work 1946-1952.* O.U.P., London, 1956

International Labour Office., *International Migration 1945-1957*, Studies and Reports, New Series No.54. I.L.O., Geneva, 1959

International Sociological Association., *The Positive Contribution of Immigrants: A Symposium*, U.N.E.S.C.O., Paris, 1955

International Sugar Council., *The World Sugar Economy: Structure and Policies,* I.S.C., London, 1963

Jupp, J., *Arrivals and Departures*, Lansdowne, Melbourne, 1966

Lawler, R., *Summer of the Seventeenth Doll*, Currency Press, Sydney, 1957

Markovic, L., *Ispod Australskog Neba*, Jugoslavenske Akademije, Znanosti, Zagreg, 1973

Martin, J.I., *Refugee Settlers: A Study of Displaced Persons in Australia.* A.N.U., Canberra, 1965

Menghetti, D., *The Red North: The Popular Front in North Queensland*, History Department, J.C.U., Townsville,1981

Naish, J., *The Cruel Field*, Hutchinson, London, 1962

Naish, J., *That Men Should Fear*, Hutchinson, London, 1963

Queensland Sugar Cane Growers' Council, *Sugar Country: History of Raw Sugar Industry of Australia 1864-1964*, Q.S.C.G.C., Brisbane, 1965

Richards, L., *Displaced Persons: Refugee Migrants in the Australian Political Context*, La Trobe Sociology Papers. Paper No.45, May 1978

Saunders, K., *Workers in Bondage: the Origins and Bases of Unfree Labour in Queensland 1824-1916*, Q.U.P., St Lucia, 1982

Scott, W. (Compiler)., *Complete Book of Australian Folklore*, Ure Smith, Sydney, 1976

Sheahan, D., *Songs from the Canefields*, Canberra Publishing and Printing Company, 1972

Sherington, G., *Australia's Immigrants 1788-1978*, George Allen and Unwin, Sydney, 1980

Singleton, F., *Twentieth Century Yugoslavia*, Macmillan, London, 1976

Stevens, B., "Immigration Policy for the Future" in Holt, H.E. (et.al.). *Australia and the Migrant*, Angus and Robertson, Sydney, 1953

Such, L., *Cane: A Book of Drawings by a Canecutter*, Gordonvale, Queensland, 1932

Vandercook, J.W., *King Cane: the Story of Sugar in Hawaii*, Harper and Bros., London, 1939

PERIODICAL ARTICLES

_____, "Advertisements", *The Producers' Review*, XL No.1, Nov 1949

A.S.P.A., *Annual Reports.* 47th Annual Report, 1955

_____, *Annual Reports.* 48th Annual Report, 1956

_____, *Annual Reports.* 54th Annual Report, 1962

_____, "Immigrant Labour in the Sugar Industry", *The Australian Sugar Journal*, XL No.7, Oct 1948

_____, "Displaced Person Migrants", *Ibid*, XL No.9, Dec 1948

_____, "Minutes", *Ibid*, XLI No.2, May 1949

_____, "Manpower for 1949 Season. Displaced Persons for Canefields", *Ibid*, XLI No.2, June 1949

_____, "Migrant Cane Cutters", *Ibid*, XLI No.3, June 1949

_____, "Small Flow of Rural Migrant Labour", *Ibid*, XLI No.10, Jan 1950

_____, "Migrant Labour Still Needed", *Ibid*, XLI No.11, Feb 1950

_____, "Manpower for 1951 Harvest", *Ibid*, XLII No.2, May 1951

_____, "Output of Australian Cane Cutters", *Ibid*, 52 No.12, March 1961

Birch, A., "The Implementation of the White Australia Policy in the Queensland Sugar Industry 1901-1912", *Australian Journal of Politics and History*, XI No.2, April-Dec 1965

Birch, A., "The Organization and Economics of Pacific Islands' Labour in the Australian Sugar Industry 1863-1906", *Business Archives and History*, VI No.1, Feb 1966

Boland, R., "A 'Fair Go' for the Cane Cocky", *North Australian Monthly*, 5 No.10, May 1959

Bolton, L., "Memories before the 18th Doll", *Cairns Post*, 12 Oct 1973

Borrie, W.D., "Economic and Demographic Aspects of Post-War Immigration to Australia", *R.E.M.P. Bulletin*, 3 No.1, Jan-March 1955

Borrie, W.D., "The Growth of the Australian Population with Particular Reference to the Period since 1947", *Population Studies*, 13 No.1, July 1959

Borrie, W.D. & Zubrzycki, J., "Employment of Post-War Immigrants in Australia", *International Labour Review*, 77 No.3, March 1958

Bottomley, C., "Sugarfield Scenes", *South West Pacific Annual*, December 1945

_____, "Canecutters' Era at End", *Courier-Mail*, 12 December 1977

_____, "Cane Cutters' Working Overtime", *Producers' Review*, XL No.8, July 1950

Curlewis, F.C.P., "The Australian Cane Sugar Industry: Its Development in Queensland", *Royal Geographical Society of Australasia* (Queensland Branch), a lecture delivered on 17 June 1936

Fitzhardinge, L.F., "Immigration Policy: A Survey", *Australian Quarterly*, 21, June 1949

Foley, L., "Five, Six, Pick Up Sticks. Innisfail has a Festival", *Bulletin*, December 1963

Gillies, F.D., "Sugar", *Economic News*, 18 No.10, Oct 1949

Gollschewsky, E., "The Yesterdays and Todays of the Sugarcane Industry", *Bulletin*, April 1969

Graham, M., "Our Canecutters", *North Australian Monthly*, 6 No.7, Feb 1960

Gray, L.C., "Economic Efficiency and Competitive Advantages of Slavery under the Plantation System", *Agricultural History*, IV No.2, April 1930

Hempel, J.A., "The Migration Problem in Queensland", *Economic News*, 21 No.3, March 1952

Jaggard, E., "Australian Immigration 1900-1950: A Survey", *Historicus*, 7, Aug 1973

Johnston, E., "Canecutters Award Whittled Down to a One-Man Stand", *Australian*, 21 December 1977

_____, "Judgement on Annual Review Claims and Week-end Penalty Rates - 3. Cases and Appeals", *Producers' Review*, XL No.6, April 1950

Kunz, E.F., "European Migrant Absorption in Australia", *International Migration*, 9 No.1-2, 1971

Kunz, E.F., "The Genesis of the Post-War Immigration Programme and the Evolution of the Tied-Labour Displaced Persons Scheme", *Ethnic Studies*, 1 No.1, 1977

Loveira, C., "Labour in the Cuban Sugar Industry", *International Labour Review*, 20, 1929

Mercer, P., "Pacific Islanders in Colonial Queensland 1893-1906", *Lectures on North Queensland History*, History Department, J.C.U., 1974

_____, "The Magic Grass", *People*, 19 February 1958

Molesworth, B.H., "Kanaka Labour in Queensland 1863-1871", *Historical Society of Queensland Journal*, 1 No.3, Aug 1917

Mollett, J.A., "Capital and Labour in the Hawaiian Sugar Industry since 1870: A Study of Economic Development", *Jour. of Farm Economics*, XLIV No.2, May 1962

Moore, C.M., "Queensland Sugar Industry from 1860-1900", *Lectures on North Queensland History*, History Department, J.C.U., 1974

Morton, C., "Sugar in North Queensland", *North Australian Monthly*, 2 No.6, Jan 1956

Morton, C., "Sugar in North Queensland: Crushing Comment", *Ibid.*, 4 No.2, Sept 1957

Morton, C., "Sugar in North Queensland: Sugarcane Waste, Fertilizer Bags and Human Canecutters", *Ibid.*, No.6, Dec 1957

Morton, C., "Sugar in North Qth Queensland: Dry-cleaned Cane is not Clean Enough", 5 No.2, Sept 1958

Mulherin, K.S., "Canecutting Awards in the Queensland Sugar Industry", *Quarterly Review of Agricultural Economics*, X No.3, July 1957

Partlow, L.L., "The Hawaiian Sugar Plantations", *Asia*, 31, Jan 1931

Pitman, F.W., "Slavery on British West India Plantations in the 18th Century", *Journal of Negro History*, 11, Oct 1926

Q.C.G.A and A.S.P.A., *The Australian Sugar Year Book*, 1956

_____, *Queensland Manufacturers Year Book*, The Strand Press, I, 1947; IV, 1950; VII, 1953; VIII, 1954

Roberts, L., "Are Canecutters a Doomed Race? What Mechanization will mean to the North", *North Australian Monthly*, 5 No.12, July 1959

Roberts, L., "Centenary Year Flashback: The Plantation Era in North Queensland", *Ibid.* 6 No.2, Sept 1959

Roberts, L., "Another of the Vanishing Australians", *Ibid.* No.4, Nov 1959

Shlomowitz, R., "Team Work and Incentives: The Origins and Development of the Butty Gang System in Queensland's Sugar Industry 1891-1913", *Journal of Comparative Economics*, 3, 1979

Simonett, D.S., "Sugar Production in North Queensland", *Economic Geography*, 30, 1954

Sires, R.V., "Negro Labor in Jamaica in the Years following Emancipation", *Journal of Negro History*, 25, 1940

Tyrell, W.B., "The Canecutters are at Work", *North Australian Monthly*, 1 No.2, Sept 1954

Wilson, J.L.T. , "Northmost Queensland", *Current Affairs Bulletin*, 12 No.12, Sept 1953

_____, "Workers' Accommodation Acts - Amendment of Regulations", *Producers' Review*, XL No.6, April 1950

_____, "Workers' Accommodations Acts, 1915 to 1946", *Ibid.* 11, Sept 1950

UNPUBLISHED MATERIAL

Bertei, J.M., Innisfail., B.A. Hons. thesis, University of Queensland, 1959

Henderson, L.D., Italians in the Hinchinbrook Shire 1921-1939, B.A. Hons. thesis, James Cook University, 1975

Jackson, W., The Government and Economic Growth in Queensland 1946-1951, B.A. Hons. thesis, University of Queensland, 1968

Kleinschmidt, M.A., Migration and Settlement Schemes and Queensland, B.A. Hons. thesis, University of Queensland, 1951

Shepherd, R.L., The Herbert River Story, Unpublished typescript. Hinchinbrook Shire Council - Historical Library